Rude Pursuits and Rugged Peaks

THE OZARKS COLLECTION

Other titles in this series

Roll Me in Your Arms: "Unprintable"
Ozark Folksongs and Folklore, Volume I

The Battle for the Buffalo River:
A Twentieth-Century Conservation Crisis in the Ozarks

Blow the Candle Out: "Unprintable"
Ozark Folksongs and Folklore, Volume II

An Arkansas Folklore Sourcebook

The White River Chronicles of S.C. Turnbo:
Man and Wildlife on the Ozarks Frontier

Ozark Vernacular Houses: A Study of Rural Homeplaces
in the Arkansas Ozarks, 1830-1930

Rude
Pursuits
AND
Rugged
Peaks

*Schoolcraft's
Ozark Journal
1818–1819*

With an Introduction,
Maps, and Appendix
by Milton D. Rafferty

THE UNIVERSITY
OF ARKANSAS PRESS
FAYETTEVILLE ✦ 1996

00 99 98 97 96   5 4 3 2 1

Designed by Ellen Beeler

⊚ The paper used in this publication meets the minimum requirements of the American
National Standard for Permanence of Paper for Printed Library Materials Z39.48-1984.

Library of Congress Cataloging-in-Publication Data

Schoolcraft, Henry Rowe, 1793–1864.
    [Journal of a tour into the interior of Missouri and Arkansaw] Rude pursuits and
rugged peaks : Schoolcraft's Ozark journal, 1818–1819 / with an introduction, maps,
and appendix by Milton D. Rafferty.
        p.   cm.
    Includes bibliographical references and index.
    ISBN 1-55728-412-1 (alk. paper)
    1. Missouri—Description and travel. 2. Arkansas—Description and travel. 3. Ozark
Mountains. I. Rafferty, Milton D., 1932-   . II. Title.
F466.S35   1996
917.7804'3—dc20   95-43009
                                                                        CIP

Contents

LIST OF ILLUSTRATIONS   vii

PREFACE   ix

INTRODUCTION   1

    THE OZARKS: THEN AND NOW   2

    PLANT LIFE   3

    LANDFORMS AND HYDROGRAPHIC FEATURES   5

    HUMAN HABITATION   6

    A CHANGING OZARKS   6

    WHO WAS HENRY ROWE SCHOOLCRAFT?   8

    SCHOOLCRAFT'S OBJECTIVES   9

    SCHOOLCRAFT'S LATER ACHIEVEMENTS   11

    REFERENCES   14

REPRODUCTION OF THE TITLE PAGE OF THE *JOURNAL*   18

THE JOURNAL

    I. FROM POTOSI TO ASHLEY CAVE   19

    II. FROM ASHLEY CAVE TO THE BEAVER CREEK SETTLEMENT   35

    III. DELAYED AT THE BEAVER CREEK SETTLEMENT   67

    IV. THE TOUR TO THE LEAD MINE ON THE JAMES RIVER   76

    V. DOWN THE WHITE RIVER FROM THE BEAVER CREEK
       SETTLEMENT TO POKE BAYOU   95

    VI. FROM POKE BAYOU TO POTOSI   113

REPRODUCTION OF THE TITLE PAGE OF "TRANSALLEGHENIA"   126

"TRANSALLEGHENIA, OR THE GROANS OF MISSOURI"   127

APPENDIX   143

INDEX   167

Illustrations

FIGURE 1. SCHOOLCRAFT'S ROUTE THROUGH THE OZARKS. 2

FIGURE 2. OZARK TOWNS AND WHITE RIVER SETTLEMENTS, CIRCA 1819. 7

FIGURE 3. HENRY ROWE SCHOOLCRAFT. 10

FIGURE 4. MAP OF THE OZARKS REGION, CIRCA 1821. 16–17

FIGURE 5. VIEW OF POTOSI. 20

FIGURE 6. TOUR ROUTE FROM POTOSI TO ASHLEY CAVE. 21

FIGURE 7. TURN-OF-THE-CENTURY LUMBERING SCENE IN THE SHORTLEAF PINE FORESTS OF SHANNON COUNTY, MISSOURI. 27

FIGURE 8. ASHLEY CAVE (SALTPETER CAVE), 1995. 30

FIGURE 9. TOUR ROUTE FROM ASHLEY CAVE TO THE BEAVER CREEK SETTLEMENT. 37

FIGURE 10. NORTH FORK OF THE WHITE RIVER, 1994. 41

FIGURE 11. FRONTIER CABIN. 53

FIGURE 12. SUGARLOAF KNOB AND SUGARLOAF PRAIRIE NORTHEAST OF LEAD HILL, ARKANSAS, 1994. 63

FIGURE 13. TOUR ROUTE FROM THE BEAVER CREEK SETTLEMENT TO THE LEAD MINES ON THE JAMES RIVER AND ON TO POKE BAYOU. 77

FIGURE 14. SMALLIN CAVE, 1995. 81

FIGURE 15. AERIAL VIEW OF LOGAN'S RIDGE, BULL CREEK VICINITY, CHRISTIAN COUNTY, MISSOURI, CIRCA 1995. 87

FIGURE 16. AERIAL VIEW OF CLEARED LAND IN THE WHITE RIVER HILLS REGION, CIRCA 1990. 91

FIGURE 17. AERIAL VIEW OF DEWEY BALD NEAR BRANSON, MISSOURI, CIRCA 1970. 92

FIGURE 18. BULL SHOALS DAM AND LAKE. 101

FIGURE 19. CEDAR GLADE WITH EXPOSED BEDROCK NEAR BULL
SHOALS, ARKANSAS, 1993. 107

FIGURE 20. CALICO ROCK AND THE WHITE RIVER, 1994. 109

FIGURE 21. TOUR ROUTE FROM POKE BAYOU TO POTOSI. 115

FIGURE 22. THE NARROWS OF THE LITTLE ST. FRANCIS
RIVER, 1995. 123

Preface

I first read Henry Rowe Schoolcraft's *Journal* as part of a geographer's preparation to live and teach in the Ozarks. For nearly thirty years, I have carried the *Journal* as I guided student field trips and traveled and explored the region to satisfy my curiosity. Schoolcraft's words are a reminder of what once was, and sadly, sometimes, of what has been lost forever. Recent growth in population and economic development has completely reshaped the local lifestyle and landscape in some sections of the Ozarks. Giant reservoirs now drown hundreds of river bottom farms, and some scenic landscapes are altered almost beyond recognition by tourism and urban growth. With this in mind, I sought to have the *Journal* reprinted for the convenience of modern readers and to better preserve one of the first records of the Ozark scene.

My task in preparing an introduction to Schoolcraft's account was multifaceted. For readers unacquainted with the Ozarks, there is a brief description of its physical and cultural attributes. Because the territory Schoolcraft described was virtual virgin wilderness, I have called attention to major elements of environmental change. I also include a brief biographical sketch of Henry Rowe Schoolcraft. Besides recounting his many notable achievements, an explanation of what Schoolcraft was doing in the Ozarks during the early 1800s is presented. I also focused on trying to map the route Schoolcraft and his companion on the tour, Levi Pettibone, most probably followed. This was sometimes difficult because the two adventurers lost their way on at least one occasion and were unsure of their whereabouts much of the time. The appendix includes commentary drawn from my field notes on the late-twentieth-century landscape and a list of county highway maps and topographic quadrangles that follow Schoolcraft's route. References are included for those who wish to read further on Henry R. Schoolcraft and the Ozarks.

Tracing Schoolcraft's route has been a longtime avocation (since 1967). While leading student field trips in the region and for personal enjoyment, I traveled by foot, automobile, and canoe over the same route Schoolcraft followed. Sometimes I returned repeatedly to certain "problem" locations with maps and *Journal* in hand in an effort to correlate Schoolcraft's text with the landscape. In this manner, I penciled my interpretation of Schoolcraft's route onto my working maps.

Every word of the *Journal* appears as published by the London printers, though I have added modern place names in brackets following the first time Schoolcraft's name for the location, if different, appears in the journal. To provide a framework for better comprehension, I have divided the journal into six parts that correspond to the detailed maps of the major segments of the tour. The map published in the 1821 *Journal* appears in its original form to provide the reader with a cartographic view of the region at the time Schoolcraft made his tour. Modern maps and photographs will help readers trace Schoolcraft's travels and better comprehend some of his verbal descriptions. Those who wish to visit specific sites described by Schoolcraft should refer to the table of topographic and county highway maps in the appendix. The third column of the table includes a day-by-day description of the modern landscape along Schoolcraft's route. It provides a basis for comparing the late-twentieth-century scene with Schoolcraft's description of the 1818–19 landscape.

Schoolcraft's account of his travels into the Ozarks first appeared under the tedious title, *Journal of a Tour into the Interior of Missouri and Arkansas, from Potosi, or Mine à Burton, in Missouri Territory, in a South-West Direction, Toward the Rocky Mountains; Performed in the Years 1818 and 1819* (London: Sir Richard Phillips and Company, 1821). For brevity, the title appears as *Journal of a Tour into the Interior of Missouri and Arkansas in 1818 and 1819,* or simply, Schoolcraft's *Journal*. The *New York Literary Journal and Belles Lettres Repository* published an earlier abbreviated version of the journal in 1821. This initial version included anecdotal material and personal commentary in an apparent effort to enliven the stark and often technical prose of his original handwritten journal. Schoolcraft apparently wrote the abbreviated version to recoup financial losses after his book, *View of the Lead Mines of Missouri,* sold poorly.

The expanded 1821 edition, reprinted here, retained the journal format and its rather terse tone, but Schoolcraft added information on vegetation and wildlife. He also described the many hardships and difficulties commonly encountered by greenhorn explorers in the backwoods. The added human interest material provided a colorful, though somewhat jaundiced, characterization of the white hunter society that had taken root in the Ozark wilderness. This version was republished in 1853, with *A View of the Lead*

Mines of Missouri as an appendix, as *Scenes and Adventures in the Semi-Alpine Region of the Ozark Mountains of Missouri and Arkansas.*

A facsimile edition, *Schoolcraft in the Ozarks* (Van Buren, AR: Press-Argus Printers, 1955), was never widely available in libraries and is now long out of print. The new edition makes Schoolcraft's journal readily accessible for the first time in more than a century.

SIGNIFICANCE OF THE JOURNAL

Schoolcraft's *Journal* was the earliest report on the interior Ozarks by a skilled observer. John Bradbury's *Travels in the Interior of America (1809-11)* was one of the first detailed descriptions of the Missouri River Valley since the publication of the findings of the Lewis and Clark expedition of 1803–6, but its descriptions of the Ozarks were limited to the river border. Likewise, Henry Brackenridge's commentaries in *Views of Louisiana (1814)* did not go beyond the towns along the Mississippi River and the Missouri lead mines. Although German adventurer and writer Friedrich Gerstacker traveled in Missouri and Arkansas in the 1830s, his observations first appeared in print many years later. In fact, Gerstacker's *Wild Sports in the Far West* originally appeared in German in 1844, more than twenty years after the publication of Schoolcraft's *Journal.* Another ten years passed before it was translated and published in English. Furthermore, Gerstacker's Ozark travels were limited to traversing the Southwest Trail through the eastern foothills and to an extended hunting trip into the Boston Mountains. Because Schoolcraft's later work gained wide recognition and the *Journal* carried the weight of being the first report on the region, it gradually achieved the status of a benchmark study. Even so, the *Journal* is not without its detractors. For that matter, much of Schoolcraft's later work suffered from a lack of originality and heavy borrowing from his own previous work and that of others. Critics have also called attention to his tendency to include redundant and unrelated material in his writing. The long, tedious poem "Transallegenia, or the Groans of Missouri," appended to the Ozark journal, is a case in point. Schoolcraft's writing, occasionally colorful, suffers at times from distracting Teutonic sentences with dependent clauses heaped one after the other.

George Lankford has criticized the *Journal's* historical reliability, taking issue with Schoolcraft's harsh criticism of the lifestyle, education, and beliefs of the frontier inhabitants. It was common practice at the time for writers reporting on the frontier to add colorful events to enhance popular interest in their work. Some of Gerstacker's humorous accounts, for example, were undoubtedly drawn from frontier folklore. However, cultural bias seems a more likely explanation for Schoolcraft's sometimes disdainful appraisal of frontier life. Considering that Schoolcraft was only twenty-five years old and freshly indoctrinated with a church upbringing, including a strong emphasis on Christian dutifulness and temperance, it is no surprise that he viewed some aspects of the frontier lifestyle with disdain. Truly his assessment of the frontier folk showed little of the penetration of a Tocqueville or Harriet Martineau, but he was hardly equipped by intellect, training, or experience to make that kind of commentary. Distracted by a desire to end the adventure as quickly as possible, Schoolcraft recorded only brief observations on frontier life along the White River. He was hurrying to return to Potosi to write his report on the mines and to return to the East. He had borrowed money from Moses Austin to make the journey and was anxious to obtain employment to pay his debts. Then, too, Pettibone was most anxious to return to St. Louis and may have goaded Schoolcraft to make haste on the return trip.

Schoolcraft's contribution to social and cultural history was pictorial rather than analytical. He saw both good and bad elements in the character of the frontier folk and in their way of life. He praised some frontiersmen for their open hospitality and criticized others for their penurious sharp dealing and failure to live up to their obligations, much as one might characterize people encountered at random today. Schoolcraft viewed the settlers' almost complete lack of education, superstitious beliefs, and lackadaisical attitude toward work from the perspective of one freshly indoctrinated with bourgeois family values that stressed hard work, achievement, and financial success. While Schoolcraft's background may have influenced his opinion of the frontier lifestyle, the soundness and usefulness of his portrayal of the frontier material culture seem valid. The *Journal*'s strength as a historical piece stems from its foundation on direct observation by a literate eyewitness. Its attention to the details of everyday life on the frontier places it in the realm of cultural history as espoused by the likes of Voltaire and American historian John Bach McMaster. Likewise, Schoolcraft's painstaking descriptions of the geographical, geological, and biotic domain make the work a benchmark report on the region's natural environment.

Many people and agencies have helped with the preparation of this new edition of the *Journal*. Agencies that provided photographs include:

the Arkansas Department of Parks and Tourism, the Arkansas History Commission, the Missouri Division of Tourism, and the State Historical Society of Missouri. The Springfield–Greene County Library loaned their original 1821 edition of the *Journal* for photocopy work. Several students and staff members at Southwest Missouri State University worked on various parts of the project. Deana Gibson provided patient and diligent help while preparing numerous drafts of the manuscript on the word processor. Rick Havel and Jeff Ikerd, staff cartographers in the Department of Geography, Geology, and Planning, drafted the computer map of Schoolcraft's route through the Ozarks. Heather Conley, a graduate student in Resource Planning, prepared the larger scale, hand-drafted maps.

A special debt of gratitude is extended to Fred Hessel and Heather Conley, graduate research assistants, for their diligent archival research both in the preparation of the working maps and in helping to compile the background information needed to locate the route Schoolcraft followed. Fred's field work and thoughtful speculation helped to shape the final decisions incorporated in the maps. I am indebted to my colleague, Professor John Catau, for his critical review of the manuscript. I also wish to thank the Southwest Missouri State University Faculty Research Committee for financial support for student cartographers and for field trips to take photographs and to verify Schoolcraft's route.

In conclusion, I recommend that the journal be read slowly, with pauses to reflect on Schoolcraft's observations and today's scene. For those who wish to follow Schoolcraft's steps, locomotion should be slow, the slower the better; and it should often be interrupted by leisurely halts to sit at vantage points and ponder the Ozarks scene then and now.

Milton D. Rafferty

Introduction

"I begin my tour where other travelers have ended theirs," were the opening words Henry R. Schoolcraft penned in his journal November 5, 1818. The next day Schoolcraft and his lone companion, Levi Pettibone, set out with a single pack horse on a ninety-day adventure through a largely uncharted territory where very few white men had traveled. Poorly equipped, with no frontier experience and only limited knowledge of the terrain they planned to traverse, Schoolcraft and his friend, a fellow New Yorker who had recently moved to St. Louis, set off on their journey just as winter winds were gaining strength. The two inexperienced adventurers wandered from ridge to ridge, forded streams, and trudged through tangled cane brakes. Often lost, they sometimes ended the day of travel hungry, wet, and cold. To bolster their meager food supplies, they hunted wild bear, deer, buffalo, and turkey. All too infrequently, they feasted on roasted beaver tail, turkey pie, and wild honey.

Schoolcraft's tour of the Ozarks, which coincided with the emergence of Arkansas as a separate territory carved out of the Missouri district of the great Louisiana Purchase, began in the frontier lead-mining town of Mine à Breton. Pronounced "Mine à Burton" by the American miners, this Missouri community was subsequently renamed Potosi. It is now the seat of Washington County. Schoolcraft's travels took him southwest across the Ozarks to the White River, and then northwest to a lead mine on Pearson Creek near present-day Springfield, Missouri. Schoolcraft returned to Potosi on February 4, 1819, after boating down the White River to Poke Bayou (Batesville, Arkansas) and then traveling northeast along the Ozark border.

Without realizing the significance of his efforts, Henry Rowe Schoolcraft managed to preserve for posterity an eyewitness account of the region's people and their environment. Schoolcraft was a keen geographical observer and noted repeatedly that much of the area offered little agricultural potential. He learned the lifestyle and economy of the frontier inhabitants by eating, sleeping, and hunting with them. Consequently, his journal includes useful insights into many beliefs and moral precepts of the early settlers.

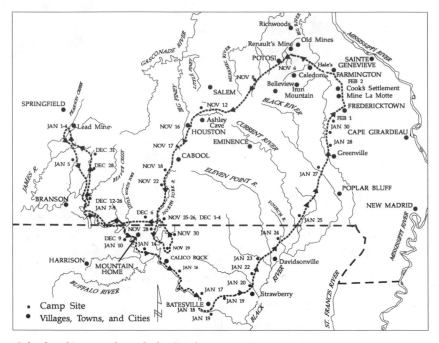

Schoolcraft's route through the Ozarks. CARTOGRAPHY BY JEFF IKERD.

THE OZARKS: THEN AND NOW

In no place in his journal does Schoolcraft refer to the region as "the Ozarks," as it is now known throughout the world. Various origins of the name have been proposed, including the fusion of the names "Osage" and "Arkansas" or the corruption of the French name for the common hedge tree, *Bois d'arc.* The most plausible explanation, documented by Carl O. Sauer in his *Geography of the Ozark Highland of Missouri,* is that the name stemmed from the common practice of the French to abbreviate place names. The French post on the Arkansas, and the river, were shortened to *aux-Arcs* or *Aux-arcs,* "to the Arkansas," or "to Arkansas Post." Sauer noted that in pioneer days the names "Arkansas" and "Ozark" were used interchangeably and were applied to the Arkansas River, its drainage basin, the highland north of it, and the post near its mouth.

The Ozark Upland extends over all or part of ninety-three counties in Missouri, Arkansas, Oklahoma, and Kansas.[*] It is bounded by the Missouri

---

[*] Milton D. Rafferty, *The Ozarks: Land and Life,* 3–6.

River on the north, the Mississippi River on the east, the Arkansas River on the south, and rolling prairies on the west. Its image, even today, is that of a poor, remote, isolated, trans-Mississippi Appalachia.

With millions of urban dwellers seeking relief from the stresses of city life in outdoor recreation, the Ozark region has become a popular tourist destination. Part of the attraction stems from the exceptional physical features that set the region apart from nearby areas. The huge billion-year-old granite boulders in the Elephant Rocks area of the St. Francois Mountains protrude through an extensive plateau comprised of nearly horizontal beds of limestone and dolomite. These rock strata extend east beyond the Mississippi River, northward beyond the Missouri River, westward into northeastern Oklahoma and southeastern Kansas, and southward into northern Arkansas. In Arkansas the igneous rocks extend under thick beds of sandstone in the Boston Mountains. Among the Ozarks' tourist attractions are many large springs and caves formed by solution of the bedrock limestones and dolomites.* Canoeists and anglers are attracted by clear, gravel-bottomed, spring-fed streams. Hikers and climbers seek out bold bluffs and wilderness areas. Tourists are drawn especially to the region's many artificial lakes and to the protected rivers set aside for canoeing and camping. Despite having been widely cut over during a forty-year timber boom that spanned the turn of the twentieth century, the Ozark forest has regenerated. Large tracts of timberland have become federal and state forests and recreation areas.

PLANT LIFE

Henry Schoolcraft and Levi Pettibone traveled through a mosaic of vegetation communities. Valley bottoms were occupied mainly by dense deciduous forest, unspoiled and virtually untouched by the imprint of human habitation. Valley walls were covered with oak, hickory, and pine forests. Uplands were covered alternately by prairie, oak savanna, oak woods with open undergrowth, and open grassy glades, or barrens.

This vast forest and woodland savanna, mainly oak-hickory and oak-hickory-pine, covered as much as eighty percent of the region. Schoolcraft noted great variation in the quality of the timber. Stands of giant oak and

---

* Areas with sinkholes, caves, and other groundwater solution features are called karst landscapes. The name stems from the Karst region of the former Yugoslavia where such features abound.

pine trees grew on the better soils, but only knurled, stunted trees could survive on the very thin, stony upland soils. Prairie openings were common on uplands. No doubt some grassy savanna-like openings grew over areas of fragipan, or mineral-cemented soil, which tree roots could hardly penetrate. Elsewhere, fertile upland soils supported lush prairies with hundreds of plant species. These may have been enlarged and maintained by the Osage people who lived and hunted in the area. A common Osage hunting technique was to purposefully set prairie fires in order to drive game into the wooded areas where the animals could be killed more easily. Some prairies in the western Ozarks were large and covered with luxuriant plant life. Schoolcraft's description of the Kickapoo Prairie captures the magnificent grandeur of the virgin prairie landscape that once occupied the upland where the city of Springfield, Missouri, now sprawls:

> The prairies, which commence at the distance of a mile west of this river [James River], are the most extensive, rich, and beautiful, of any which I have ever seen west of the Mississippi river. They are covered by a coarse wild grass, which attains so great a height that it completely hides a man on horseback in riding through it.

The upland prairies, like the river bottomlands, were later cleared of timber and planted to corn, cotton, and small grains. Today thousands of dairy and feeder cattle graze on fescue and the other domestic grasses that now cover many uplands and most river bottoms. Many other grassy savannas have been invaded by brush and scrubby timber.

Schoolcraft encountered many cedar balds and glades and commented on their open barren appearance. These natural open areas in the forest reflected a harsh yet fragile environment. They were composed of patches of exposed bedrock and shallow stony soils covered with clumps of tall prairie grasses, wildflowers, desert cacti, and stunted cedar trees. Most hilltop balds and upland glades escaped cultivation due to their poor soils.

River valleys supported a dense growth of tall cane. The cane, identified by Schoolcraft as *Cinna arundinacea,* grew so rank and tall on the fertile alluvial soils that the bottomlands were avoided by the two travelers when possible. These same cane-choked bottomlands, which later produced corn and other field crops, are now mainly fenced hay meadows.

LANDFORMS AND HYDROGRAPHIC FEATURES

Since the Ozark region is one of America's foremost karst landscapes, it is not surprising that Schoolcraft stumbled across several caves during his three-month journey. Caves, sinkholes, springs, and other solution features form easily in the thick limestone and dolomite formations. Schoolcraft had knowledge of Ashley Cave (Saltpeter Cave) near Montauk Spring and took refuge there for three nights during a prolonged downpour. Near present-day Ozark, Missouri, he stumbled across Smallin Cave (Civil War Cave) and noted that its remarkable entrance occupied the entire width of the stream valley.

Prominent hills served as guideposts for Schoolcraft as they did for the hunters who traversed the Ozarks. Isolated hills were especially conspicuous landmarks when they protruded above the forest and were without trees. Two such isolated "bald knobs," Sugarloaf Knob and Helphrey Hill, were significant for Schoolcraft and Pettibone in their travels in the White River hills. A mixture of bunch grass, cedar, and scrubby oak now mantles most of the former bald hills. This is most likely due to the decline of annual burning of pastures and glades.

Schoolcraft's descriptions of Ozark rivers and streams are particularly vivid. The sheer river bluffs cut by meandering rivers impressed him. Some bluffs, Calico Rock on the White River for example, served as landmarks for river travelers. It is curious, though, that despite his many references to stream crossings, Schoolcraft mentioned stream gravels only casually. Perhaps this is evidence that Ozark waterways carried much less rock in former times, as recorded by some observers. No doubt much of the great load of gravel now so characteristic of Ozark streams was washed from steep hillsides after the forests were cut and the soils cultivated.

Shoals were hazards to river travel, but remarkable in their beauty and the incessant roar of the water crashing through the boulder strewn chutes. These river rapids formed where streams cut into a particularly resistant layer of rock. Schoolcraft's journal entry of his trials in passing through the Bull Shoals on the White River is all that remains of these rapids; they now lay deep below the water of Bull Shoals Lake.

Schoolcraft passed close to several large springs without knowing of them. Even so, the two travelers had little trouble finding water for drinking and cooking due to the great abundance of springs. Only occasionally during the three-month tour did Schoolcraft complain of having to make a dry camp.

HUMAN HABITATION

Although the French had established outposts in the mid-Mississippi Valley at Kaskaskia and Kahokia in 1699 and at St. Louis in 1763, white settlement in the Ozarks was still in its infancy when Schoolcraft and Pettibone began their trip. The old French lead-mining settlements at Mine La Motte, St. Michael's, Bonne Terre, and Mine à Breton were just beginning to grow and spread as American miners and farmers entered the region. Even so, settlement had hardly spread beyond the eastern river valleys and the mining districts. Agricultural settlements occupied most of the favorable sites along the Mississippi and Missouri Rivers. Farms were prospering on the fertile limestone soils of the Fredericktown and Farmington basins and in the Bellevue and Arcadia Valleys in the St. Francois Mountains. Settlement was spreading along most of the larger river valleys in the eastern Ozarks as well. Schoolcraft noted the many new barns and houses along the St. Francis River and most of the other rivers he crossed on the return trip from Arkansas to Potosi.

A handful of the hardiest woodsmen, those cut from the same cloth as Daniel Boone and his sons, had settled along some of the interior streams where they made their living hunting and trading with the Osage. It was this latter type that Schoolcraft encountered along the White River. He described in detail their food, clothing, tools, weapons, cabins, and furniture. Schoolcraft admired their stoic courage and tenacity, but could not conceal his disdain for their lack of education and rude lifestyle. He noted that men and women alike could talk only of bears, hunting, and the rude pursuits and coarse enjoyments of hunters. Despite their "disgusting, terrific, rude, and outré" behavior, lack of deep religious convictions, and their burdensome superstitions, the settlers displayed an open hospitality.

A CHANGING OZARKS

One hundred seventy-five years and an additional two million inhabitants have wrought great changes in Ozark geography and landscape. For many years following Schoolcraft's exploratory tour the Ozarks remained a back-

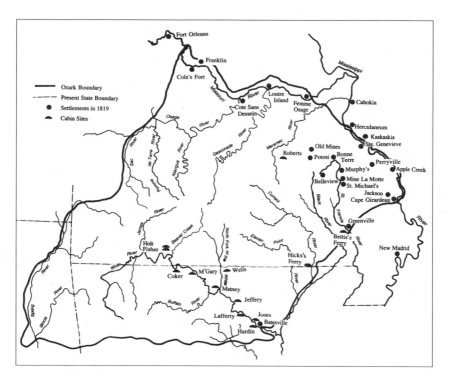

Ozark towns and White River settlements, circa 1819. Adapted from George Lankford, "'Beyond the Pale': Frontier Folk in the Southern Ozarks," and Milton Rafferty, Historical Atlas of Missouri. CARTOGRAPHY BY HEATHER CONLEY.

woods area affected only marginally by the growth and development that occurred in other areas of the country. Even so, by the 1880s railroads tapped the region's forest and mines. Highways soon followed the railroads, and dams formed a dozen large artificial lakes. Towns grew up in the mining districts, along the railroads, at river fords, at road junctions, and on lake shores. A few strategically located places have become small cities.

Modernity first followed the rails and then the roads. Lumbering, mining, and manufacturing brought investment, jobs, and new people. Commercial dairy, fruit, and livestock farms replaced the traditional subsistence farms. The railroads also stimulated the first tourism in the form of spa hotels and hunting and fishing camps. Large dams created more than 7,350 miles of lake shoreline. Fear of more dams led to the protection of the most pristine and beautiful rivers. Tourism, second-home development,

rapidly rising land prices, and explosive population growth all blend into
the modern Ozarks scene.

Now, three-quarters of a century after the large lumber mills closed, the
forests have regenerated—not to their primeval magnificence but sufficient
enough to support sustained-yield lumbering and a large wildlife population. Deer and turkey abound. The wily black bear roams over a wider range
each year. Many towns that grew rapidly during the halcyon days of mining
and lumbering (only to later slowly decline) are once again growing under
the stimuli of tourism and retirement living. Today, when scenery, water, and
recreational potential attract millions of visitors, the Ozark region is again
experiencing an era of rapid growth and development. It is, in many ways,
a region whose time has come.

The most remarkable change over the past 175 years is the great increase
in the number of inhabitants with their amazing variety of cultural traits,
beliefs, and lifestyles. The backwoods hunters Schoolcraft encountered on
the White River were submerged by a wave of hardy newcomers who farmed
or worked in the mines and forests. A combination of successive waves of
immigration, and great improvements in the region's economic and educa-
tional opportunities, have greatly altered the Ozarks' traditional lifestyles. The
old pattern of life based on farming and working in the timber and mines, supported by a stable social system of close family ties, small rural churches and
schools, and limited outside contacts, is changing rapidly. Expectations for
improved economic well-being have increased. Women have left the unpaid
home or farm workplace and have entered the commercial workplace; the two-
income family is now commonplace. Diminished poverty and the virtual dis-
appearance of the distasteful imagery of the lethargic "hillbilly" have reshaped
the region's image. Even so, it is the possibility of glimpsing these largely
departed lifestyles that holds an intrinsic fascination for many visitors.

WHO WAS HENRY ROWE SCHOOLCRAFT?

Many years before New York publisher Horace Greeley admonished young
easterners to "go west" to seek their fortunes, thousands of young men,
including Henry Schoolcraft, turned to the American West for a fresh start.
The economic collapse of the wood-fired glass industry in the Northeast,
an embarrassing bankruptcy stemming from the subsequent closing of the
Ontario Glass Works in which Schoolcraft was a partner, Schoolcraft's interest in writing, and his perception that money could be made by compiling

accounts about the western frontier led him to explore the Ozark Region in 1818–19 and the Upper Great Lakes Region in 1820–21. There was a strikingly economic bent in all of his endeavors. For example, his examination of the lead-mining region of Missouri, including studying the methods of mining and smelting, the tenure of leases, and the transportation aspects of the industry, led him to think he could receive an appointment as a federal superintendent of the area's mines.

Schoolcraft was born on March 28, 1793, in Albany County, probably in the little town of Watervliet (now Guilderland Village), on the Hudson River in New York State. He attended schools at Hamilton, New York, and later pursued studies of chemistry and mineralogy with Professor Frederick Hall at Middlebury College in Vermont.

Schoolcraft seemed possessed by geology. Rocks had been a common childhood novelty, and his work as superintendent of a glass factory required a professional knowledge of mineralogy. While in Missouri he enlisted the aid of Moses Austin's miners as he collected various mineral specimens. His enthusiasm for mineral treasures stimulated the composition of a dreadfully dull poem, "Transallegania, or the Groans of Missouri," which he included in the original *Journal* (see pp. 126–42).

His middle-class English and German parents indoctrinated Schoolcraft with devotion to hard persistent work. While other young men were attending horse races, cockfights, and other amusements, Henry usually stayed home to work on his studies. His biographer paints a picture of a dull, driven young man with a consuming desire and natural flair for writing. Unfortunately, the opportunity to elevate and enhance his gift for writing with formal instruction at nearby Union College in Schenectady was lost when the business at his father's factory declined. Instead of college training Lawrence Schoolcraft sponsored his son's practical education by steadily increasing his responsibilities at the glass factory.

SCHOOLCRAFT'S OBJECTIVES

When placed within the context of his lifetime activities and accomplishments, Henry Rowe Schoolcraft's three month Ozarks expedition in the winter of 1818–19 was a small episode, almost a youthful adventure. Even so, the notes he recorded and later organized and published as a journal preserved one of the few contemporary records of the natural setting and the manner of frontier settlement during its earliest stage of development.

Henry Rowe Schoolcraft. COURTESY OF THE STATE HISTORICAL SOCIETY OF MISSOURI.

Schoolcraft was only twenty-five years of age when he journeyed to the Ozarks from his home in western New York seeking a fresh start. He traveled by flatboat and keelboat from New York to St. Louis, then struck out overland to Potosi, arriving in August 1818.

While staying at the home of Moses Austin in Potosi during September and October, Schoolcraft conducted a detailed survey of the mining and smelting operations and visited with the principal miners within a radius of forty miles. After hearing reports of lead deposits on the James River in the southwestern Ozarks, Schoolcraft began planning an excursion to the area. He persuaded several backwoodsmen to accompany him on the trip, but by the date of departure all but Levi Pettibone had backed out.

Schoolcraft admitted that he and Pettibone were utter neophytes in woodsmanship, campcraft, and hunting when they set out on their journey. They anticipated "living off the land" by killing game for sustenance, but their shotguns were unsuited for killing large animals. While they may have chosen the short-range guns because of their lack of skill with a rifle, they soon learned from the wife of a hunter that a rifle was essential for the hunting of deer, bear, elk, and buffalo. Some of Schoolcraft's information about the Ozarks may have come from reports of travelers who had passed by the region's margins, but the limited information about the interior surely came from hunters and miners who had ventured into the rugged hill districts.

His expedition into the interior Ozarks was unquestionably directed at the lead deposits twenty miles above the junction of Finley Creek and the James River branch of the White River. When Schoolcraft reached this site, he built a temporary shelter and remained for several days while investigating the lead deposits. After leaving the Pearson Creek camp, he returned to Potosi by the most rapid and expeditious route. The first report on his Ozark experiences, *A View of the Lead Mines of Missouri*, was rushed into print so Schoolcraft could take copies to Washington, D.C., and persuade Congress to create a federal superintendency for the Missouri mining districts.

SCHOOLCRAFT'S LATER ACHIEVEMENTS

Although his main goal to be appointed as a mining superintendent failed, Schoolcraft gained considerable notoriety as a mineralogist through publication of *A View of the Lead Mines of Missouri*. His reliable information about the geology and natural history of the American West, as well as his firsthand knowledge and his collection of mineral specimens, gained him early access to many important men of science. Schoolcraft also sent copies of the book to such luminaries as President James Monroe, Secretary of War John C. Calhoun, Missouri Senator Thomas Hart Benton, and Vice President Daniel Thompkins.

The notoriety gained from his book, coupled with his lobbying efforts in Congress and the strong support of the secretary of war, led to Schoolcraft's appointment as the mineralogist and naturalist for the Cass Expedition to the region around Lake Superior and the Upper Mississippi River. Schoolcraft's success in assisting with Indian negotiations and in subsequent Indian councils led to his appointment as secretary of a commission to treat with the Indians at Chicago. So successful was he in his dealings with them that in 1822 he was named Indian agent for the tribes in the Upper Great Lakes Region, and he established his headquarters at Sault Ste. Marie. There he built the agency house of some fifteen rooms and in 1823 married Jane Johnston, a one-fourth Chippewa Indian and granddaughter of the noted Ojibwa Chief Waboojeeg. From the agency headquarters at Sault Ste. Marie, and later on Mackinac Island, with the assistance of his wife, Schoolcraft began assembling, recording, and collating a monumental collection of Indian lore. He became a recognized authority on Indian history, language, and customs. In addition to serving as his link into the society of Sault Ste. Marie, Jane was also his direct source for much of the Indian myth and legend that he wrote about so voluminously.

His accumulation of manuscript notes on Indian customs and language increased with each passing day of contact with Indians visiting at the agency. Also, his involvement in frontier affairs continued to expand. He served in the Michigan territorial legislature, founded the Michigan Historical Society, helped to establish the Algic Society in Detroit, and was awarded a medal by the French Institute for his lectures before the Algic Society on *The Grammatical Construction of the Indian Language,* which had been translated into French. In 1832 Schoolcraft was selected to lead the government expedition up the Mississippi River to its source in Itasca Lake. In 1836 he negotiated a treaty with the Indians on the Upper Great Lakes that led to the cession of sixteen million acres for eventual settlement by whites. In 1845, following the death of his wife and a trip to Europe, he served as a commissioner to take a census of Indians in New York and to collect information on the tribes banded together under the name "Six Nations."

The paradox of Schoolcraft's life is that at the same time he was recording the vanishing culture of the Chippewa Indians of the Algonquin Nation, he was also helping to formulate many of the policies that would ultimately destroy the very civilization he studied so intensely. Eventually, he secured funds from Congress to publish the voluminous information he had collected in six separate volumes under the title *Historical and Statistical Information Respecting the History, Condition and Prospects of the Indian Tribes of the United States*. Even when his body was wracked with age and restricted mobility, he struggled to convince members of Congress to appropriate the funds needed to publish the Indian history. Thanks in large part to the help of his second wife, Mary Howard Schoolcraft, the massive work was published.

Schoolcraft's biographer asserts that he carried an innate ambition to be a literary figure along with his reputation as a geologist and ethnologist. In all he wrote thirty-one larger works and many more short articles. He was honored by membership in several scientific societies and in 1846 was awarded the honorary LL.D. degree from the University of Geneva. Writers often used his material for their own stories: Longfellow is said to have created Hiawatha out of one Schoolcraft report.

Henry Rowe Schoolcraft died penniless on December 10, 1864. Richard Bremer notes that Schoolcraft's life offers insights into the phenomenon of the self-made man in the turbulent society of nineteenth-century America. A tremendous underlying motivation and resolve carried him through a series of major setbacks that included: the deaths of his firstborn son, his beloved brother, and his first wife; repeated financial losses; charges of misuse of government funds and the hiring of relatives; and a series of strokes that left him a bedridden cripple.

While there was strong economic motivation in virtually all of his endeavors, Schoolcraft's major goals were the achievement of public recognition and the approval of his work by the scientific community. In retrospect, his life seems tortured, tragic, and sad in many respects. A deep-rooted and pervasive sense of insecurity made Schoolcraft a driven man. In his constant quest for recognition and economic security, he tried hard to win the approval of others, including his social and political superiors and authority figures such as his father. Unfortunately, his aloofness and his tendency to stand on dignity when challenged left him with few true friends.

While he wrote prolifically for forty years, some of his works contained material taken from other published sources. His later works often contained segments of his earlier manuscripts in an altered or untouched form. Even so, his great accomplishment was that he became a leading authority in the study of Indian language and folklore.

REFERENCES

Bowen, Francis. "Schoolcraft on the Indian Tribes." *North American Review* 77 (1853): 245–62.

Brackenridge, Henry M. *Views of Louisiana, Together with a Voyage up the Missouri River, in 1811*. Chicago: Quadrangle Books, 1962.

Bradbury, John. *Travels in the Interior of America*. Ann Arbor, Mich.: University Microfilms, 1966.

Bremer, Richard G. *Indian Agent and Wilderness Scholar: The Life of Henry Rowe Schoolcraft*. Mount Pleasant, Mich.: Clarke Historical Library, Central Michigan University, 1987.

Chapman, C. H., and E. F. Chapman. *Indians and Archeology of Missouri*. Columbia: University of Missouri Press, 1983.

Clokes, Richard M. *William C. Ashley: Enterprise and Politics in the Trans-Mississippi West*. Norman: University of Oklahoma Press, 1980.

Cunningham, R. J., and C. Houser. "The Decline of the Missouri Ozark Forest Between 1820 and 1920." In T. A. Waldrop, ed., *Proceedings of the Conference on Pine-hardwood Mixtures*. U.S. Department of Agriculture, Forest Service, Southeastern Forest Experiment Station, 1989.

Featherstonehaugh, G. W. *Excursion Through the Slave States, from Washington on the Potomac to the Frontier of Mexico, with Sketches of Popular Manners and Geological Notices*. New York: Harper and Brothers, 1844.

Fenneman, N. M. *Physiography of the Eastern United States*. New York: McGraw-Hill, 1938.

Freeman, John Finley. "Henry Rowe Schoolcraft." Ph.D. diss., Harvard University, 1959.

Gerstacker, Friedrich. *Wild Sports in the Far West*. Durham, N.C.: Duke University Press, 1968.

Jacobson, Robert B., and Alexander T. Primm. *Historical Land-use Changes and Potential effects on Stream Disturbance in the Ozark Plateaus, Missouri*. U.S. Geological Survey Open-File Report 94-333. U.S. Geological Survey, Denver, Colorado, 1994.

Keefe, James F., and Lynn Morrow. *The White River Chronicles of S. C. Turnbo: Man and Wildlife on the Ozarks Frontier*. Fayetteville: University of Arkansas Press, 1994.

Ladd, Douglas. "Reexamination of the Role of Fire in Missouri Oak Woodlands." In *Proceedings of the Oak Woods Management Workshop*. Charleston, Ill.: Eastern Illinois University, 1991.

Lankford, George E. "'Beyond the Pale': Frontier Folk in the Southern Ozarks." *The Folk: Identity, Landscapes, and Lore*, edited by Robert J. Smith and Jerry Stannard. University of Kansas Studies in Anthropology, no. 17. Lawrence, Kans., 1989.

McCarty, J. Kenneth. "The Ozarks of Henry Rowe Schoolcraft: A Land that Used to Be." *Ozarks Watch,* 6, nos. 1 and 2 (summer-fall 1992): 30–37.

Mason, Phillip P., ed. *Schoolcraft's Expedition to Lake Itasca: The Discovery of the Source of the Mississippi.* East Lansing: University of Michigan Press, 1958.

Nigh, Tim, and Larry Houf. "In the Footsteps of Henry Rowe Schoolcraft: A View of the Ozarks in the Early 1800's." *Missouri Conservationist* 54 (May 1993): 9–15.

Osborn, Chase S., and Stellanove Osborn. *Schoolcraft-Longfellow-Hiawatha.* Lancaster, Penn.: n.p., 1942.

Park, Hugh, ed. *Schoolcraft in the Ozarks: Reprint of Jornal of a Tour into the Interior of Missouri and Arkansas in 1818 and 1819.* Van Buren, Ark.: Press-Argus, 1955.

Pettibone, Levi. "With Schoolcraft in Southwest Missouri in 1818." *Missouri Historical Society Collections* 2 (1900): 46–51.

Rafferty, Milton D. *The Ozarks: Land and Life.* Norman: University of Oklahoma Press, 1980.

—— *Historical Atlas of Missouri.* Norman: University of Oklahoma Press, 1981.

—— *The Ozarks Outdoors: A Guidebook for Fishermen, Hunters, and Tourists.* Norman: University of Oklahoma Press, 1985.

Sauer, Carl O. *Geography of the Ozark Highland of Missouri.* The Geographic Society of Chicago Bulletin 7. Chicago: University of Chicago Press, 1920.

Schoolcraft, Henry R. *A View of the Lead Mines of Missouri.* New York: Arno Press, 1972.

—— *Journal of a Tour Into the Interior of Missouri and Arkansas in 1818 and 1819.* London: Sir Richard Phillips and Company, 1821.

Steyermark, J. A. *Vegetational History of the Ozark Forest.* University of Missouri Studies, vol. 31. Columbia, Mo., 1959.

Williams, Meed C. "Henry R. Schoolcraft." *Missouri Historical Collections* 2 (1903): 45–57.

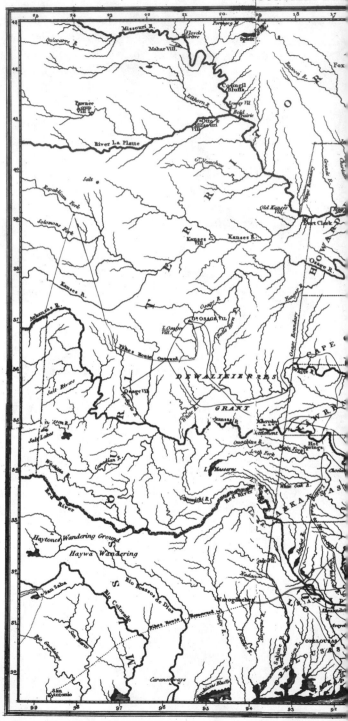

*Map of the Ozarks
Region, circa 1821.*

REPRINTED FROM
SCHOOLCRAFT'S *JOURNAL.*

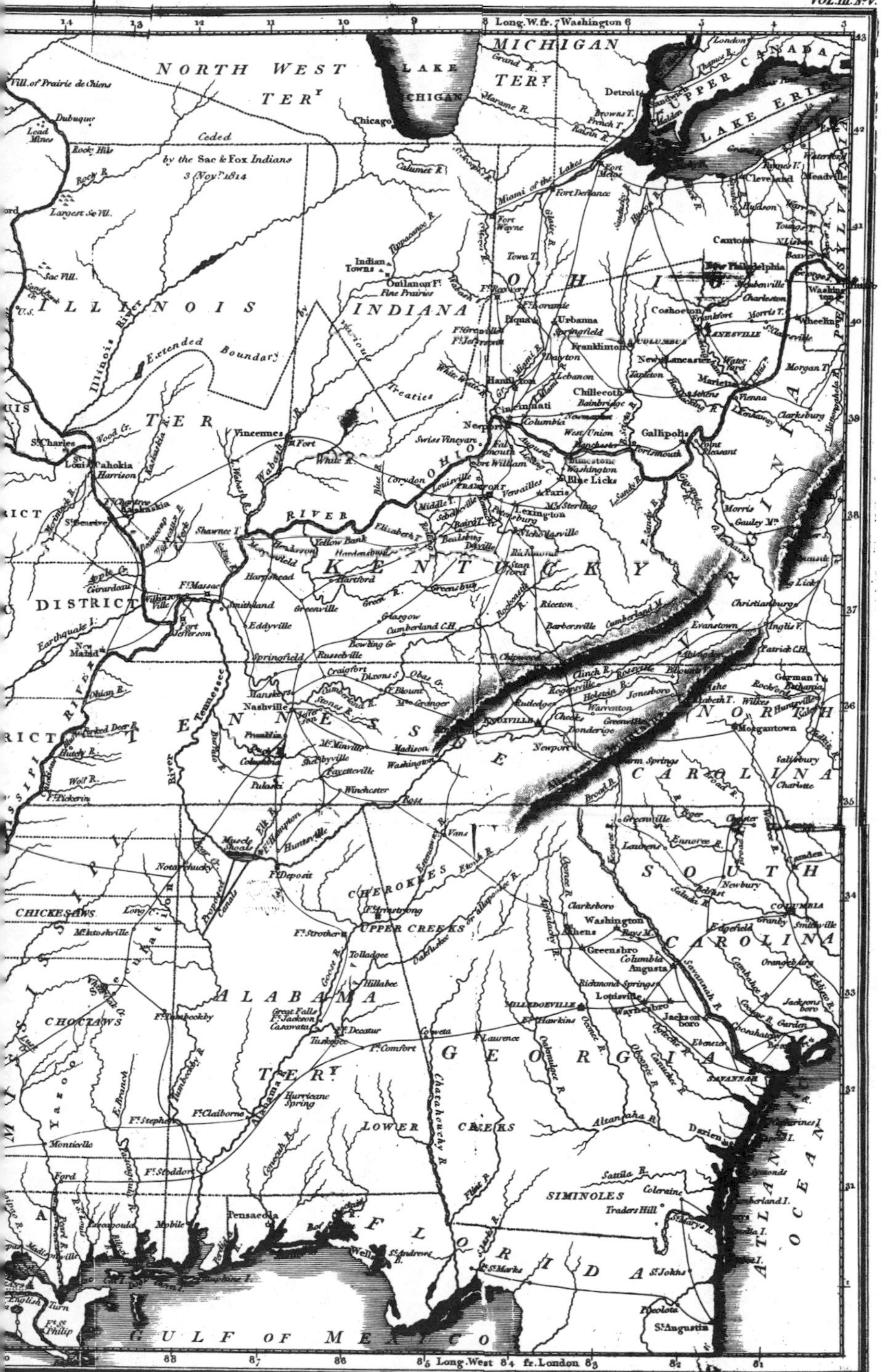

NORTH WEST TERY

MICHIGAN TERY

LAKE MICHIGAN

UPPER CANADA

LAKE ERIE

Detroit

Chicago

Ceded by the Sac & Fox Indians 3 Novr 1814

ILLINOIS

INDIANA

OHIO

Cincinnati

COLUMBUS

VIRGINIA

Wheeling

Vincennes

OHIO RIVER

Frankfort

Lexington

KENTUCKY

Nashville

TENNESSEE

Knoxville

NORTH CAROLINA

Charlotte

CHICKESAWS

CHOCTAWS

CHEROKEES

UPPER CREEKS

ALABAMA TERY

GEORGIA

SOUTH CAROLINA

COLUMBIA

Augusta

Savannah

LOWER CREEKS

SIMINOLES

FLORIDA

St Augustin

Pensacola

Mobile

ATLANTIC OCEAN

GULF OF MEXICO

Long. West fr. London

JOURNAL

OF

A TOUR

INTO

THE INTERIOR OF MISSOURI AND ARKANSAW,

FROM

Potosi, or Mine à Burton, in Missouri Territory, in a South-West Direction, toward the Rocky Mountains;

PERFORMED IN THE YEARS 1818 AND 1819.

By HENRY R. SCHOOLCRAFT.

LONDON:

PRINTED FOR SIR RICHARD PHILLIPS AND Co.

BRIDE-COURT, BRIDGE-STREET; AND TO BE HAD OF ALL BOOKSELLERS.

1821.

I

From Potosi to Ashley Cave

POTOSI, THURSDAY, 5TH NOV. 1818.

I begin my tour where other travellers have ended theirs, on the confines of the wilderness, and at the last village of white inhabitants, between the Mississippi river and the Pacific Ocean. I have passed down the valley of the Ohio, and across the state of Illinois, in silence! I am now at the mines of Missouri, at the village of Mine à Burton, (now called Potosi,) and surrounded by its mineral hills and smoking furnaces. Potosi is the seat of justice for Washington county, Missouri territory, and is situated forty miles west of St Genevieve, and about sixty south-west of St. Louis, the capital. It occupies a delightful valley, of small extent, through which a stream of the purest water meanders, dividing the village into two portions of nearly equal extent. This valley is bordered by hills of primitive limestone, rising in some places in rugged peaks; in others, covered with trees, and grouped and interspersed with cultivated farms, in such a manner as to give the village a pleasing and picturesque appearance. It contains seventy buildings, exclusive of a court-house, a jail, an academy, a post-office, one saw, and two grist mills, and a number of temporary buildings necessary in the smelting of lead. In its vicinity is found a considerable tract of very fertile land, and a lively interest is manifested to the pursuits of agriculture; but the trade of Potosi is chiefly in lead, which is, in a great degree, the medium of exchange, as furs and peltries formerly were in certain parts of the Atlantic states. Very great quantities of lead are annually made at this place, and waggoned across the country to the banks of the Mississippi, a distance of forty miles, for

View of Potosi. COURTESY OF THE STATE HISTORICAL SOCIETY OF MISSOURI.

shipment. It is estimated that, from the year 1798 to 1816, 9,360,000 pounds of lead were smelted here. There are about forty mines in this vicinity. The price of lead is 4 per cwt. in the pig. The ore worked is galena, or sulphuret of lead, which is found in abundance, and smelts very easily, yielding from sixty to seventy per cent. of metallic lead in the large way. It is found in alluvial soil, along with sulphate of barytes [barites], radiated quartz, and pyrites, and also in veins in primitive limestone.

FRIDAY, NOV. 6TH.

Having completed the necessary preparations, I left Potosi at three o'clock, P. M., accompanied by Mr. Levi Pettibone, being both armed with guns, and clothed and equipped in the manner of the hunter, and leading a pack-horse, who carried our baggage, consisting of skins to cover us at night, some provisions, an axe, a few cooking utensils, &c. On walking out of the village of Potosi, on the south-west, we immediately commenced ascending a series of hills, which are the seat of the principal mines, winding along among pits, heaps of gravel, and spars, and other rubbish constantly accumulating at the mines, where scarcely ground enough has been left undisturbed for the safe passage of the traveller, who is constantly kept in peril by unseen excavations, and falling-in pits. The surface of the mine-hills is, in fact, completely perforated in all directions, although most of the pits have not been continued more than twenty or thirty feet below the surface, where the rock has opposed a barrier to the further progress of the miner. On reaching the summit of these hills, we turned to survey the beautiful prospect behind us, the valley of Potosi, with its village and stream, the cultivated fields on its borders, the calcareous hills crowned with oaks beyond, with the distant furnaces smoking through the trees, and the wide-spread ruins at our feet. A deep blue sky hung above us; the atmosphere was clear and pure, with a gentle breeze from the south-west, which, passing through the dried leaves

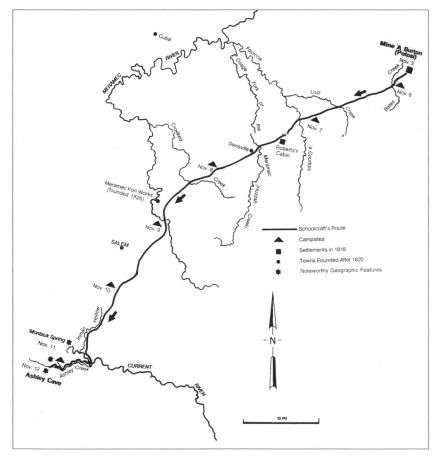

Tour route from Potosi to Ashley Cave. CARTOGRAPHY BY HEATHER CONLEY.

of the trees, scattered them over the valley we had left, and murmured a pensive farewell. We turned to pursue our way with such feelings as many travellers have experienced on turning their backs upon the comforts and endearments of life, to encounter fatigue, hard fare, and danger. On travelling three miles from this spot, we arrived at a deserted Indian cabin on the banks of a small stream called Bates' Creek, where we determined to encamp for the night.

SATURDAY, NOV. 7TH.

As we are unacquainted with the hunter's art of travelling in the woods, we shall necessarily encounter some difficulties from our want of experience, which a hunter himself would escape. We find it necessary to gain a knowledge of things, of which we before knew nothing, and in which we had not any experience, such is the art of hobbling a horse properly, with safety to ourselves, and without injury to him—the best method of building a camp fire—how to cook a piece of venison, or boil a pot of coffee, &c. Such are now the objects which will engross our daily attention, and to excel in which becomes a point of ambitious exertion. An instance of our inexperience in these particulars occurred this morning. Our horse, owing to a defect in hobbling, went astray during the night, and we consumed the day until 10 o'clock, in hunting him up, when we repacked our baggage, and continued our way in a south-west direction toward the Fourche à Courtois [Courtois Creek]. After travelling fourteen miles, the day being nearly spent, we arrived at an inhabited cabin, and obtained permission to remain for the night. Our path this day has lain across an elevated ridge of land, covered with yellow pine, and strewed with fragments of sandstone, quartz, and a species of coarse flinty jasper, the soil being sterile, and the vegetation scanty. The weather has been mild, and very pleasant for the season, with an unclouded sky, and light breeze from the south-west. General course of travelling west-south-west. Distance, fourteen miles.

SUNDAY, NOV. 8TH.

In travelling two miles this morning, we found ourselves on the banks of the Fourche à Courtois, a considerable stream, and one of the principal tributaries of the Merrimack river [Meramec River]. The Fourche à Courtois originates in high lands near the head of the river St. Francis, and after running in a serpentine course for sixty miles, through a sterile country, unites with the Merrimack 100 miles from its mouth. Its banks, at the place we crossed, afford some very rich lands, but they do not extend far, consisting merely of a strip of alluvion [alluvium] running parallel with the river, and bordered by hills, whose stony aspect forbids the approach of the farmer. On this stream are settled several persons, who divide their time between hunting and farming. The district of tillable land is much more extensive, however, than has generally been supposed, and is capable of supporting a considerable population, which will, eventually enhance the agricultural character and importance of that part of Washington county. We had proceeded but a short distance beyond the Fourche à Courtois, when the barking of dogs in a contiguous forest, announced our approach to a hunter's cabin, where we halted to inquire respecting the Indian trace to the country of the Osages, which we were informed ran in the direction we were travelling, and might be pursued for sixty or seventy miles with advantage. The owner of the cabin was not himself in when we first arrived, but his wife very readily gave us every information respecting the direction of the trace, the streams we were to cross, the game we might expect to find for our subsistence, and other particulars, evincing a perfect acquaintance with the subject, adding, that it was dangerous travelling in that quarter on account of the Osages, who never failed to rob and plunder those who fell in their way, and often carried them in captivity to their villages, on the Grand Osage river. She said her husband had contemplated going out on a hunt into that quarter for several days, but was fearful of going alone lest he should fall in with a party of those Indians; but she thought he would be willing to accompany us a part of the way, and advised us to await his return from the woods, as he had only gone a short distance to kill some turkey. While we were waiting his return, she continued to repeat several incidents of robberies and murders committed by the Osages, and unusual hardships which had been encountered in the woods by her husband and others. She told us, also, that our guns were not well adapted to our journey; that we should have rifles; and pointed out some other errors in our dress, equipments, and mode of travelling, while we stood in astonishment to hear a woman direct us in matters which we had before thought the peculiar and exclusive province of men. While thus engaged the husband entered, and readily agreed to our proposal, to accompany us toward White River, where he represented the game to exist in great abundance. In a few moments he was ready. Putting three or four large cakes of corn-bread in a sack, and shouldering a rifle, he mounted his horse, and we all set forward together, mutually pleased with the reciprocal benefits expected from travelling in company. Our path, for the first four miles, lay across a succession of sterile ridges, thinly covered with oaks, when we suddenly descended into the valley of the Osage Fork of the Merrimack [Huzzah Creek], a stream equal in size to the Fourche à Courtois, and having extensive prairies all along its banks. On this stream we passed through a small village of Delaware Indians, who are now all out hunting, except the old men, women, and children. Four miles below the spot where we crossed this stream, is situated a large village of the Shawanees, and three miles above is another settlement of Delawares.

On leaving the valley of Osage Fork, we immediately entered on a hilly barren tract, covered with high grass, and here and there clumps of oak-trees. Soil poor, and covered with fragments of jaspery flint, horn-stone, quartz, and detached masses of carbonate of lime. Such, indeed, has been the character of the small stones under foot from Potosi, but the ledges breaking out on hill sides have uniformly been limestone, stratum upon stratum.

We encamped after dark in a small valley near a spring. Distance eleven miles.

MONDAY, NOV. 9TH.

The sleep of the hunter is not sound, neither is his vigilance to be eluded; and the anxiety he is kept in, from the fear of the Indian on the one hand, and the approach of wild animals on the other, produces constant wakefulness during the night. His horse and baggage also demand occasional notice during the darkness of night, and he lies down with his rifle in his arms, to be prepared for emergencies. An instance of this vigilance occurred last night, and prevented a loss which would, in our situation, have been irreparable. Our packhorse, who, as usual, was turned loose to graze, accompanied by that of the hunter, strayed off from our camp, but was not long gone, when missed by Roberts, (the hunter,) who awoke me, and we pursued, and overtook them about three miles off, and brought them back to camp before day-light. All this serves to increase our caution; and the farther we proceed, the more serious would be any loss we might sustain, either in our horse, guns, locks, ammunition, or any other article necessary to our safety or subsistence. During the night we had several times been disturbed

by the approach of elk and deer, and as soon as the day dawned, Roberts
went out a short distance and killed a fine fat doe, which he brought in on
his shoulders, and we made a breakfast, for the first time, on roasted deer's
meat, with appetites sharpened by exercise, which, while it invigorates the
body, as we experience, increases its alimentary capacities. Our route this
day has been over barrens and prairies, with occasional forests of oak, the
soil poor, and covered with grass, with very little under-brush. As evening
approached we entered the valley of Merrimack, which we followed up for
several miles, and encamped in a prairie near its source. Some good bottom
lands are found on its banks, but the adjoining hills are stony and barren,
covered with little timber and high grass. Within a mile of its banks, on the
Indian trace, we passed over large beds of iron ore, accompanied by the
black oxyd [oxide] of manganese, specimens of which I take along. The
Merrimack is the only considerable stream which enters the Mississippi on
the west from the mouth of the Missouri to the mouth of St. Francis, a distance of nearly 500 miles. It is 200 miles in length, and joins the Mississippi,
eighteen miles below St. Louis, where it is 200 yards in width. Its depth is
not great, being only navigable fifty miles with common-sized boats, except
in the spring and fall, when its principal tributaries may be ascended. It
waters the country of the lead-mines, and affords some facilities for the transportation of lead to the Mississippi, which do not appear to be generally
known or appreciated, and have not been improved.

The weather this day has been mild and pleasant, with a light breeze
from the south-west, and a smoky atmosphere. Course of travelling south-
west, until we struck the Merrimack; then due-south, to the place of our
encampment. Distance eighteen miles.

TUESDAY, NOV. 10TH.

We packed our horse this morning at day-light, notwithstanding the rain
which commenced last evening, and continued at intervals during the night.
On travelling about ten miles, we left the Osage trace, which began to diverge
too far north, and struck through the woods in a south course, with a view
of reaching a large saltpetre cave known to exist in that quarter. Shortly after
we quit the Indian trace, Roberts, who was in advance on our left about half-
a-mile, fired at, and killed a deer, and immediately reloaded his rifle, pursued, and fired again, telling us to continue, as he could easily, being on
horseback, overtake us. We accordingly pursued our route until night, and

are now encamped on the banks of a small lake, in a prairie containing several small ponds or lakes, not having yet been rejoined by our hunter. One of the greatest inconveniences we experience in travelling in this region, arises from the difficulty of finding, at the proper time, a place of encampment affording wood and water, both of which are indispensable. On this account we find it prudent to encamp early in the afternoon, when we come to a spring of good water, with plenty of wood for fire, and grass for our horse; and, on the contrary, are compelled to travel late at night in order to find them. This is a difficulty which attends us this evening, having been compelled to stop in an open prairie, where wood is very scarce, and the water bad—general course of travelling south—weather pleasant, the rain having ceased shortly after day-light. Lands poor; trees, oaks; game observed, deer and elk. Distance twenty miles.

WEDNESDAY, NOV. 11TH.

While lying before our camp-fire last night, the wolves set up their howling, apparently within 200 yards of us. We had already been long enough in the woods, and were sufficiently conversant with the hunter life, to know that this animal will only attack men in cases of the most extreme hunger; and as we knew their common prey, the deer, was abundant in that quarter, we had little apprehension for our safety. We thought it prudent, however, to be on the watch; a thing, indeed, which we did almost every night, particularly when the cold was such as to render it necessary to keep up a fire. In these cases we slept and watched alternately, as well from a regard to safety as to mend our fire. Such, however, was the fatigue of a day's long march, that we both fell into a sound sleep for the greater part of the night, and found our fire nearly out, and ourselves chilled with cold when we awoke, the wolves being still on an adjacent hill. A short time before day-light we arose, renewed our fire, and prepared breakfast, and commenced our journey at an early hour, holding a south course across the prairie of Little Lakes. At the distance of two miles we passed a stream running south-east, and originating in the prairie of lakes. Ducks are in great plenty on this stream as well as upon the lakes. I take this to be the origin of Black River. Our route lay for the first eight miles across a barren prairie country, with little wood and no water; we then entered into lofty forests of pine, and after winding along through valleys and deep defiles of rocks for several miles, found ourselves on the banks of Current's River [Current River], in a deep and romantic valley, the soil rich, and covered with a heavy growth of trees.

Turn-of-the-century lumbering scene in the shortleaf pine forests of Shannon County, Missouri. COURTESY OF THE STATE HISTORICAL SOCIETY OF MISSOURI.

Current's River is one of the principal tributaries of Black River, and is a stream of 250 miles in length, and affords, in its whole course, extensive bodies of fertile land. Near its junction with Black River, about 200 miles below, are several settlements, and a ferry is kept ten miles above its mouth, where the Arkansaw road crosses it, and where a town is in contemplation. The waters of this stream are very clear and pure, and ducks are very common upon it. The wild turkey and grey squirrel are also seen on its banks. Five miles beyond Current's, night overtook us, and we encamped on the banks of a creek, near Ashley's salt-petre cave, in a dark, narrow, and lonesome little valley, where the rocks hung in terrific piles above our heads. Course of travelling south-west. Weather mild and smoky. Distance twenty miles.

THURSDAY, NOV. 12TH.

We find ourselves in a highly interesting section of country, and which affords some of the most picturesque and sublime views of rural scenery which I have ever beheld. The little brush camp we hastily erected last night, and in which I now write, is situated in a beautiful valley, on the banks of a small clear stream, with a rocky and gravelly bottom. The width of this valley is about 800 yards, and is bounded on the west by a perpendicular wall of limestone rock 200 feet in height, and rising in some places in cubical masses, resembling the mouldering towers of some antique ruin. On the east the bluffs are neither so high nor precipitous, and are intersected by hollows worn out of the rock by the action of rain operating, for many centuries, on calcareous rock. Down one of these hollows we descended into the valley, not, however, without leading our horse in the most cautious and circuitous manner. The top of these bluffs supports a substratum of a very sterile, gravelly alluvion, and is covered by tall pines, which add much to the beauty of the prospect from the valley below. In the stupendous wall of rocks before me are situated several caves, whose dark and capacious mouths indicate their extent. Many of these, however, cannot be visited without ladders, as they are situated forty or fifty feet above the level of the creek. With considerable difficulty and labour we entered one of them, by means of a large oak which had fallen partly against the mouth of the cave. We found it a spacious chamber, connected with others of less size, and affording both *stalactites,* and *stalagmites.* The former hang like icicles from the roof in various fanciful forms, and some specimens which we succeeded in detaching were translucent, and exhibited much beauty and regularity in the arrangement of their colours, consisting of concentric lines of yellow and brown passing by imperceptible shades into each other. We also obtained in this cave native salt-petre, very white and beautiful. It was found filling small crevices in the rock. The number of caves which we have this day visited, large and small, is seven, and all afford salt-petre. In the largest of these, great quantities of this article are annually collected and manufactured by Col. Ashley, of Mine à Burton, and transported to his powder-manufactory, in Washington county. The cavernous nature of the country bordering this stream is one of its most distinguishing characteristics, and I have seized upon this fact in calling it Cave Creek [Ashley Creek]. This little stream is one of the most interesting objects in the natural physiognomy of the country, which we have thus far met with, and affords a striking instance of that wonderful arrangement in the physical construction of the surface of the earth, which gives vallies to the smallest streams, and tears asunder rocks to allow them passages into rivers, and through them into their common basin, the ocean. Its banks rise in majestic walls of limestone, which would form the most ample barrier to the waves of the sea, and they occasionally rise into peaks, which if located on the coast of the ocean, would be hailed as landmarks by the mariner. The opposite banks correspond with general exactness in their curves, height, composition, and thickness of strata, and other characters evincing their connexion at a former period. Yet the only object apparently effected by the separation of such immense strata of rocks, a change which I cannot now contemplate without awe and astonishment, is to allow a stream of twenty yards across a level and undisturbed passage into the adjacent river, the Currents, which it joins, after winding in the most circuitous manner about four miles below. In the course of this distance, the views which are presented are commanding and delightful, and to the painter who wishes to depict the face of nature in its wildest aspect of rocky grandeur, I could recommend this valley, and the adjacent county, as one of unrivalled attractions. A scene so full of interest could not fail to receive the homage of our admiration, and we rambled about the country, until night almost imperceptibly approached, when we returned to our camp, repacked our horse, and moved up the valley of Cave Creek, one mile to Ashley Cave, in which we encamped safe from the weather, turning our horse loose to feed about its mouth. We had just built our night-fire as it became dark, and while I spread out our skins and prepared for sleep, Mr. P. boiled our accustomed pot of coffee, and got ready a supper, which, although not consisting of many dishes, or choice cookery, excited our most cordial approbation, and we partook of it with that keen appetite, and that feeling of lordly independence, which are alone felt by the wild Indian, and the half-starved Missouri hunter. Having finished our frugal meal, we determined to explore the cave before we lay down, lest some beast of prey, hid in its recesses, should be aroused by our intrusion, and pounce upon us during the night.

This cave is situated in a high wall of lime-stone rock, forming the southern bank of Cave Creek [North Ashley Creek], eighty miles south-west of Potosi, and near the head of Current's River, one of the principal tributaries of Black River, in Missouri territory. The entrance to it is by a winding footpath from the banks of the creek, and leads to the mouth of the cave at an elevation of about fifty feet above the level of the water. Its mouth is about ninety feet wide and thirty in height, a size which, without great variation, it holds for two hundred yards. Here it suddenly opens into a room which is an irregular circle, with a height of eighty or ninety feet, and a diameter of three hundred, having several passages diverging from it in various directions. The two largest passages lead south-west and south, and after winding along a considerable distance, in the course of which they are successively

Ashley Cave (Saltpeter Cave), 1995. PHOTOGRAPH BY EMMA JEAN RAFFERTY.

widened and narrowed, unite and lead on in a south course about five hundred yards, where the passage is choked up by large masses of stalactite, formed by the water which has filtered through the superincumbent rock at that place. The largest passage from the circular amphitheatre of the cave diverging north, opens by another mouth in the rock, facing the valley of Cave Creek, at no great distance below the principal mouth by which we entered. Several smaller passages diverge from each of the main ones, but cannot be followed to any great extent, or are shut up by fragments of the fallen rock. Near the centre of the largest opening, a handsome spring of clear water issues, from which we procured our water while encamped in the cave.

The ragged faces and hanging position of many parts of the sides and roof of this cave, added to its sombre colour, which has been heightened by soot smoke, its great extent, singular ramifications, and the death-like stillness which pervades such ample spaces situated so far below ground, inspire both wonder and awe, and we did not return from our examination, without feeling impressions in regard to our own origin, nature, and end, and the mysterious connection between the Creator of these stupendous works and ourselves, which many have before felt, but none have yet been satisfied about. In contemplating this connection, we feel humiliated; human reason has no clue by which the mystery may be solved, and we imperceptibly became silent, absorbed in our own reflections. Such at least was the effect produced in this instance, and we returned to trim our night-fire and go to sleep, with the taciturnity of the American savage.

FRIDAY, NOV. 13TH.

The atmosphere threatening rain this morning, we did not think proper to quit the cave, and have divided our time between hunting, mending our clothes, and noticing the geological character of the adjacent region. In hunting large game we are not very successful; our guns, as we were informed by the hunter's wife at Fourche à Courtois, not being adapted to killing deer and bear. Of wild Turkey, ducks, and squirrels, we, however, kill a plenty, to answer our purposes, and we do not seek any thing further. The most remarkable fact respecting the cave in which we are encamped, is the nitre which it yields. This is found in the native state, filling small crevices in the rock, and also in combination with the earth which forms the bottom of the cave. The nitre is formed by mixing this earth with a certain quantity of wood ashes, and lixiviating the whole in the common way by means of a tub and fasset. The potash of the wood-ashes is necessary to enable the salt to form, and the whole is then concentrated by boiling in a kettle, and afterwards set aside to cool and to crystallize. In this way the crude nitre is obtained, which may be brought to any required state of purity by redissolving and recrystallizing.

The works which have been erected by Colonel Ashley for this purpose are all situated in the mouth of the cave, so as to be completely protected from the weather. No person is, however, here at the present to attend to his business, and the works appear to have lain idle for some time. Large quantities of crude salt-petre are lying in the fore part of the cave.

The earth found in this cave, and which is now so highly charged with nitrous salts, presents an extraordinary circumstance for the consideration of the geologist, and one which must be conclusive in regard to the antiquity of the cave itself. This earth is a mixture of clay and sand in rather gross particles, but has sufficient tenacity to adhere in lumps when dug up, and contains plentifully interspersed pebbles of quartz, slate, granite, and other stones, and also fragments of horn-stone, or a kind of flint. It is in fact precisely the same kind of earth, deposited in the same manner, and mixed with the same stony substances, as the alluvion deposit which covers all the adjoining hills, and has constituted the soil of all the uplands from Potosi; nay, from the west banks of the Mississippi river to this place. The conclusion is irresistible, that this cavity in the rock existed previous to the deposition of the substratum of the soil upon the calcareous rock of this country, and, consequently, previous to the existence of trees or vegetation of any kind, unless it be of certain mosses and lichens which flourish upon naked rocks. And that when this soil was deposited, the cave in which we now sit, a pre-existing cavity in the rock, was also filled, partly or entirely, with the alluvion now found in it. The greater part of this alluvion has been subsequently washed out, and the cavity thus re-opened by water filtering through its calcareous roof, leaving certain parts on the bottom, and huge piles in several places, not situated in the current of the stream, remaining. This operation has not, indeed, wholly ceased at the present time, for the water is continually carrying down small particles of earth into the valley below, and the effect must be more perceptible after violent or long-continued rain, when the earth becomes soaked, and the infiltration of water is consequently greatly increased.

This opinion is further corroborated by observing that the sides and the root [sic, roof] of the cave, and the several passages leading from it, are water-worn, and full of smooth circular cavities like the rocky margin of the sea, or the calcareous banks of a river, and evince the force of a more powerful action than would probably be excited from any springs or streams which issue, or have ever issued from the cave. It is highly probable, therefore, that these impressions are oceanic, and existed previous to the cave's being filled with alluvial earth, and were made by that deluge of water which geologists teach us has repeatedly inundated the earth in its primeval ages, and which we have the authority of Moses for declaring did inundate the earth as late as the days of Noah.

The geological character of the country in this vicinity is secondary; the rock formations, far and wide, being secondary limestone, stratum superstratum. This has, indeed, characterized our route from Potosi to this place, with the exception of a vein of sand-stone, which alternates with it near the Fourche à Courtois. Its mineralogical character has consequently presented a corresponding uniformity, and the actual number of species and varieties of minerals found is small. Ores of iron and manganese, pyrites, quartz, horn-stone, and jasper, are the principal substances noticed. The last-mentioned mineral is found in the west bank of Cave Creek, about a mile below our present encampment. It occurs as a stratum below secondary lime-stone, by which it is overlayed to the thickness of at least 100 feet. It is the striped variety, the colours being blue and white, of various shades.

SATURDAY, NOV. 14TH.

A rain-storm which commenced during the night, has continued with little intermission, all day, so that we have been confined to the cave. Thus situated, beyond the boundaries of the civilized world, shut up in a dreary cavern, without books to amuse the mind, or labour to occupy the body, we have had ample leisure to reflect upon the solitude of our condition, and in reverting to the scenes of polished life, to contrast its comforts, attractions, and enjoyments, with the privations and danger by which we are surrounded. There springs, however, a pleasure from our very regrets; we are pleased in reflecting on scenes of former gratification; of lands that are distant, and of times that are past; and the mind is insensibly led to hope for their repetition. We expect much of the future time; we please ourselves with fond anticipations of joy, and with proud hopes of wealth, power, or renown. Thus it is that the mind is never in a state of satisfied repose, and the whole sum of human bliss is made up by the recollections we borrow from the past, and the expectations we entertain of the future. The present is never a season of happiness, which is a relative enjoyment, and can only be estimated by its absence. Neither are our ideas of this grand pursuit of our lives at all definite. Nothing can be more discordant and contradictory than the different notions which different persons or people have attached to the term happiness. One places it in wealth, another in power, a third in splendour, and a fourth in the contempt of all. Perhaps the sum of human bliss was as correctly estimated by the South Sea Indian, as it is frequently done by his more enlightened European brethren. A South Sea Indian becoming tired of life, put an end to it, by stabbing himself to the heart. The deed excited universal horror, and the grief of his family was uncontrolable. "Alas," cried a relative, "what evil spirit could have prompted him to this deed! He was blessed beyond many of his countrymen. Had he not always plenty of train-oil for his subsistence? Had he not a smooth white fish-bone, twelve inches long, run through his nose? What more could be wanting to complete his happiness?"

We have been in the expectation, for several days, of being joined by the hunter who accompanied us from the Fourche à Courtois, and who parted with us on the 10th instant, in pursuit of a deer; but night has again overtaken us, and we are again disappointed, from which it is concluded that he has either been taken prisoner by the Osage Indians, or got lost in the woods.*

* This turned out to be the fact, as we learned upon our return. Having got into a district of wood where deer were plenty, and unwilling to lose the opportunity of killing them, although he wanted neither their flesh or skins, for he could carry neither with him, he fired at, and killed many, and pursued them a great distance from the spot where we parted, and he was unable afterwards to find his way back. He wandered about nearly a week in the woods in search of us, and at last accidently arrived at the saw mills on the Gasconade river, the only settlement in that region, from which he returned in safety to his house on the Fourche à Courtois.

II

From Ashley Cave to the Beaver Creek Settlement

SUNDAY, NOV. 15TH.

This morning, the sky being clear, and the weather pleasant, we left the cave, and resumed our journey toward the south-west. On quitting the cave, our design was to turn immediately from the valley of the creek, but we found the hills so precipitous, that we were compelled to pursue up the valley, in a north-west course, for a considerable distance, before an opportunity for leaving it presented. We now entered on a high, rough, and barren tract of country, consisting of a succession of ridges running nearly at right angles to the course we travelled, so that for the first six miles we were continually climbing up slowly to the tops of these lofty heights, or descending with cautious tread into the intervening gulfs—an exercise which we found equally hazardous and fatiguing. For this distance the soil was covered thinly with yellow pine, and shrubby oaks, and with so thick a growth of underbrush as to increase, very much, the labour of travelling. To this succeeded a high-land prairie, with little timber, or underbrush, and covered with grass. We found the travelling upon it very good, although it occasionally presented considerable elevation, and inequalities of surface, and we pursued our way with a pace accelerated by the reflection that we had emerged at last from the region of stony precipices and brambled valleys, through which we had been tearing our way, at the two-fold expense of great bodily fatigue, and such parts of our clothing as were not buckskin. In calling this a high-land prairie, I am to be understood as meaning a tract of high-land generally level, and with very little wood or shrubbery. It is a level woodless barren covered with wild grass, and resembling the natural meadows or prairies of the western country in appearance, but lacks their fertility, their wood, and their remarkable equality of surface. In travelling across such a district of country, we have found little to interest. There are no prominent features in the physiognomy of the country to catch the eye. There is no land-mark in perspective, to which, by travelling, we seem to approach. The unvaried aspect of the country produces satiety. We travelled diligently and silently. Now and then an oak stood in our path; sometimes a cluster of bushes crowned the summit of a sloping hill; the deer frequently bounded on before us; we sometimes disturbed the rabbit from its sheltering bush, or were suddenly startled by the flight of a brood of quails; but there was nothing else to interrupt the silence of our march, or, by exciting fresh interest, to lighten its fatigue. The mineralogy of the country was wholly uninteresting. Its geological character presented great uniformity, the rocks being secondary limestone overlaying sand-stone. In travelling twelve miles we came to the banks of a small stream, (the first running water seen since leaving the cave,) and encamped upon its banks, just as night closed around. Distance eighteen miles.

Monday, Nov. 16th.

Nothing worthy of remark in the physical productions of the country has this day been met with. The face of the country, soil, trees, animals observed, and weather, have presented no character different from what was noticed yesterday.

We quit our encampment at early day-light, taking a due south-west course by the compass. In travelling five miles we came to a stream, running north-west, from which we conclude it is tributary to the Missouri. In fording it, I observed the bottom to be a grey compact of sand-stone, while its banks, in common with all the adjacent region, are secondary lime-stone. This sand-stone appears to be, in fact, the rock upon which the great secondary lime-stone formation of this country rests. It has appeared as the lowest stratum in almost every high bluff, and forming the surface of almost every deep valley, from the banks of the Mississippi at the cornice rock, a little below Herculaneum, to the place of our present encampment, a distance in a south-west course of about 150 miles. How far it extends south and west it is impossible to say. Every appearance tends, however, to justify an opinion, that it reaches far to the west, and that it overlays those

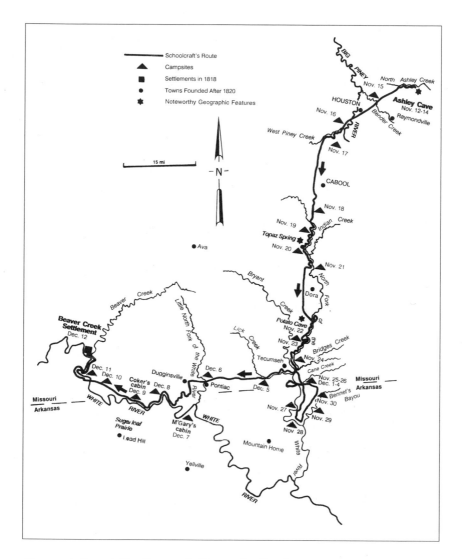

Tour route from Ashley Cave to the Beaver Creek settlement.
CARTOGRAPHY BY HEATHER CONLEY.

primitive rocks which are supposed to extend eastwardly from the rocky mountains. Four miles beyond this stream we arrived on the banks of another, and a larger stream, running also toward the north-west, and spent several hours in attempting to cross it. We succeeded at last in getting our baggage and our horse safely over, at the expense only of the time we had lost, and a handsome wetting. Three miles farther brought us to the banks of the third stream, little inferior in size to the one last passed, and winding off also in a general course toward the north-west. Upon the banks of this stream we encamped for the night, the afternoon being nearly spent, and feeling somewhat fatigued from the labour of crossing so many streams, and tearing our way through the brush and green-briar so thickly interwoven on their borders, while the intervening ridges were little else but a pile of angular stones, with here and there an oak-tree, set as if all the ingenuity of the stonemason had been exercised upon it. When the Edinburgh Reviewer estimated that Louisiana only cost three cents per acre, on the average of the whole number of square miles in the territory, he probably had no idea that there was any part of it which could be considered dear at that price. Yet, I think it would be money dearly expended in the purchase of such lands as we have this day traversed. Distance twelve miles.

TUESDAY, NOV. 17TH.

We have been at a loss to know what river the streams we yesterday passed are tributary. Their course shows them to belong to the Missouri, through some of its lowermost southern tributary rivers. We conclude ourselves too far south for the Gasconade, and that we have consequently fallen upon the head waters of the Little Osage. This opinion is strengthened by the distance we have travelled, and by our having previously passed what we considered as the head waters of the Gasconade. If on the Little Osage we are farther north than we wish, and, under this impression, we this morning altered our course from south-west to south-south-west, which carried us directly up the valley of the creek on which we encamped. In travelling two or three miles, however, it bent off too far west, and we again entered upon the highlands. We had not travelled far when we discovered, in a ravine below, four bears upon trees. We have not heretofore sought to go out of our way for the purpose of hunting, but this was directly in our course, and too fine an opportunity to exercise our skill in hunter sport to be neglected. We accordingly determined to give them battle. To prevent the effects of a fright, we tied our horse to a sapling, and putting balls on top of the charge already in our fowling-pieces, began cautiously to get within shooting distance. Unluckily we had no dog, and as the country was open, the bears soon perceived us. The only hope now was to run immediately to the foot of the trees to keep them up; but while attempting this, they began, one after the other, to come down; my companion sprained his ankle in running, and fell, while I arrived within fifty yards of the tree, and had the mortification to snap my gun at the last one, just as he had gained the foot of the tree. They fled across an adjacent ridge, and we in pursuit, but the tall grass screened them from our sight; and, after spending an hour in fruitless search, gave up the chase, returned to bring up our pack-horse, and pursued our way, considerably fatigued by an adventure, in which the bears certainly were victorious. The most serious evil, however, was to come. Pettibone had sprained his ankle, but not conscious of the hurt at first, had considerably inflamed it in the pursuit of the bear. He now began to feel its effects, and in travelling two miles farther, the pain became so severe, that he was unable to proceed, and we encamped in a valley, where we found both wood and water, at about two o'clock in the afternoon. Distance six miles.

WEDNESDAY, NOV. 18TH.

On our stopping yesterday to encamp, my first care, after unpacking the horse and turning him loose to feed, was to erect a snug camp, for I expected my companion would be confined several days by the hurt he had received. The pain seemed intense, so that he was unable to stand. We were not prepared for such an accident, our whole medicine-chest consisting of a box of Lee's pills, and some healing-salve. I recommended, however, the only thing I thought might be beneficial that our travelling pack afforded. It was a solution of common salt in warm water. With this we bathed the ankle, and bound it up with flannel and buffaloe-skin. This done, and a good log-fire built in front of the camp, he had all the physical aid which could be given; and, while he sought repose on a bed of skins resting upon dry grass, I took my gun and strolled about the valley within hearing of camp, with the view of killing some birds for supper. This was in reality one of the most pensive moments I experienced in my whole tour. The reflection that we should be confined a week or fortnight at that spot, where there was not green herbage enough for our horse to subsist, where there were neither deer or wild turkey, where there happened to be very little wood contiguous to the camp, and which was, altogether, a most dreary and desolate place; all this served to stamp the accident as a peculiar misfortune, and my anxiety was increased, by the knowledge that we had not provisions enough killed to last half that time; and by the fear that the inflammation, which was severe, might terminate, through the want of medical aid, in a mortification, and endanger his life. Such reflections obtruded themselves, while I sauntered around on the desolate rocks overlooking our camp. The fact is, I killed nothing, but was rejoiced on my return to find that the pain was not so violent. He took a cup of strong coffee and a biscuit for supper, and after enjoying a good night's rest, awoke in the morning, greatly improved. He could stand upon his foot, and thought, by a different arrangement of our pack, he might ride the horse, and continue our journey. That arrangement was accordingly made; and, mounting the horse, he seated himself on the top of our blankets and skins, and we bid adieu to our camp, with spirits as much exhilarated above the common tune, as they had, the evening before, been depressed below it. Our course of travelling was south-south-west, which carried us directly up the valley. We had not, however, gone more than a mile when two bears were discovered, at no great distance, playing with each other in the grass. We were, in fact, within shooting distance, and had approached without exciting either notice or alarm. Mr. P. for a moment forgot his pains, and dismounted to take a shot at them. We each put an additional ball into our guns, and examined our priming; then taking a deliberate aim, both fired at the same moment. Neither shot took effect, or if wounded, they ran with their usual clumsiness over an adjoining hill, leaving us the satisfaction of having shot at a bear.

We now entered on a very elevated tract of land, barren in appearance, but still covered with oaks, and rising one ridge above another, until we had attained a very great elevation, and one which commanded the most extensive prospect to the north and north-west; and, on gaining its summit, the view was equally commanding to the south and south-east. This ridge appears to be a favourite haunt for elk and bear, which have been frequently seen in our path. The enormous size of the horns of the elk give that animal an appearance of singular disproportion, but it has a stately carriage, and in running, by throwing up its head, brings the horns upon its back, which would otherwise incommode, if not entirely stop, its passage through a thicket. On descending from this highland, we came upon the banks of a small stream running south, and which originated in several springs in the valley which we have thus accidentally struck. Presuming it to be a tributary of White River, we pursued down its banks for about six miles and encamped. Distance eighteen miles.

THURSDAY, NOV. 19TH.

The valley we are now in is bounded on each side by bluffs of lime-stone overlying sand-stone. The mineralogical character of the country has been quite uninteresting since last noticed. From this spot we shall no longer travel by the compass, but pursue the stream, which I shall for the present call Limestone River [North Fork of the White River], in all its windings down. This stream is wholly composed of springs which gush at almost every step from its calcareous banks, and it rapidly assumes the character of a considerable river. The waters are very pure, cold, and transparent. We have this day passed over some rich bottom lands, covered with elm, beech, oak, maple, sycamore, and ash. We have frequently driven the deer from its covert; and the wild turkey, duck, and grey squirrel, have been almost constantly in sight. General course south. Distance twelve miles.

FRIDAY, NOV. 20TH.

Within a mile from our last night's encampment, we met with the first cane, and found new difficulties in forcing our way through it. Our approach to a warmer climate is further indicated by several green plants which we have not before noticed, and particularly by the black haw, which we have this day found in great perfection, notwithstanding the advanced season. The

North Fork of the White River, 1994. PHOTOGRAPH BY MILTON RAFFERTY.

lands continue to be that rich alluvion which is common to all the streams and vallies of Missouri, and covered by a luxuriant growth of forest-timber, shrubs, vines, cane, and green-briar, often so matted and interwoven together, that our progress is not only retarded, but attended with great fatigue. The extent of these bottoms is, however, small, and they are bordered by very high bluffs of calcareous rock. In our progress, we have been continually breaking in upon the retreats of those natural possessors of the soil, the bear and the deer. The turkey, the duck, swan, prairie-hen, and squirrel, have also viewed us as enemies, and fled at our approach. Such is the admirable power and foresight with which the Creator has endowed every part of animated nature, for its own conduct and preservation, that whether operating by instinctive impulse, as in the deer or wild-fowl, or by a reasoning and comparing faculty as in man, the effect is equally powerful, certain, and complete.

The stream which we are pursuing is devious beyond all example, and is further characterized by being made up wholly of springs, which bubble up from the rocks along its banks. No tributary has, as yet, swelled its current, either from the right or the left; but it continues visibly to increase from the springs, some of which are of immense size, and all remarkable for the purity of their waters. We have passed one of these springs to-day, which deserves to be ranked among the natural phenomena of this region. It rushes out of an aperture in a lime-stone rock, at least fifty yards across, and where it joins the main river, about 1,000 yards below, is equal to it, both in width and depth, the waters possessing the purity of crystal. I set my gun against a tree, and unbuckled my belt, preparatory to a drink, and in taking a few steps towards the brink of the spring, discovered an elk's horn of most astonishing size, which I afterwards hung upon a limb of a contiguous oak, to advertise the future traveller that he had been preceded by human footsteps in his visit to the Elkhorn Spring [probably Topaz Spring].

The difficulties we find in making our way down this valley, especially with a horse, seem to increase with the size of the stream, and the width of the valley; and if we formerly thought it wearisome in climbing over stony ridges, we now find it laborious in breaking our way through thickets bound together by grape-vines and green-briar, which are constantly either entangling our horse's feet, or become so wound around our bodies, that we are obliged to use a knife in cutting through. In breaking through one of these thickets I lost my mineral hammer, a misfortune I shall have frequent cause to regret, as it served both for detaching small specimens of such mineral bodies as I found worthy of notice, and for occasionally putting a nail in the shoes of our horse. The latter is, I confess, the only essay I have ever had occasion to make in the farrier's art; but it is an attention dictated by humanity, and which every traveller who makes long journeys across such stony and desolate tracts, should be provided for. We encamped at dusk on the brink of the river, on the skirts of an extensive cane-brake, more fatigued than we have been for several days, and having only travelled a distance of twelve miles. General course, south.

SATURDAY, NOV. 21ST.

The bottom-lands continue to improve both in quality and extent, and the growth of cane is more vigorous and green, and affords a nutritious food for our horse. The bluffs on each side of the valley continue, and are covered by the yellow pine. At the distance of six miles below our last night's encampment, the river receives its first tributary from the left in a stream of a size nearly equal to itself, which enters at the foot of a very lofty bluff, nearly at right angles, and the river below their junction is visibly increased in size. The extreme limpidity of the water of this stream gives rise to a species of deception of which we have this day had a serious proof. It is so clear, white, and transparent, that the stones and pebbles in its bottom, at a depth of eight or ten feet, are reflected through it with the most perfect accuracy as to colour, size, and position, and at the same time appear as if within two or three feet of the surface of the water. Its depth cannot, therefore, be judged by the eye with any probability of that degree of exactness which can be had by looking into common clear streams. The explanation of this phenomenon is referable to the extreme degree of the purity of the water, which holds no fine particles of earth in suspension, and admits the rays of light to pass through it without being intercepted or refracted by those particles.

In attempting to ford the river where the water appeared to be two, or at most three feet deep, the horse suddenly plunged in below his depth, and was compelled to swim across, by which our baggage got completely wetted. Our tea, meal, salt, sugar, &c. was either greatly damaged, or entirely spoiled; our skins, blankets, and clothing, were also soaked with water, and such part of our powder as was not bottled shared the same fate. This proved a serious misfortune, as our situation precluded the possibility of getting new supplies. It was near night when this accident happened, and we immediately encamped, and began to dry our effects, and save what was not wholly ruined, in which we consumed a considerable part of the night. The weather continues mild and pleasant. We have passed innumerable flocks of turkey in the course of this day: also bear, deer, pigeon, duck, and squirrel. General course, south-south-east. Distance twelve miles.

Sunday, Nov. 22d.

The difficulties attending our process along the banks of the river induced us this morning to take the highlands, where we found the travelling much easier, both to ourselves and our horse. On quitting the valley of the lime-stone we held a due-west course for about two miles, in order completely to disengage ourselves from the pine-forest, the ravines, and the brush, bordering the right bank of the river, when we found ourselves on an open barren, with very little timber, or under-brush, and generally level. We now altered our course to south-south-west, and travelled in a direct line fourteen miles without meeting any thing worthy of remark. We passed over a sterile soil, destitute of wood, with gentle elevations, but no hills or cliffs, and no water. The want of the latter we began sensibly to experience as night approached, and entered a rocky valley bending towards the south-east in hopes of finding it. Nothing could equal the sterility, or the rugged aspect of this valley, which deepened rapidly as we went, and was nothing more than a dry channel scooped out of a mass of rocks and stones, and seemed alike to forbid the expectation of finding either wood, grass, or water. For two miles we pursued our way without the prospect of finding a suitable place to encamp. Night was closing fast around us, and as the sky darkened, the wind began to rise, and as it murmured among the pines which crowned the high bluffs by which we were encompassed, seemed to forbode that we were destined to pass a cheerless night. We almost involuntarily stopped to survey the scene around us, and at this moment observed a small spring of water trickling among the stones at our feet; and turning toward its source, a cave [probably Potato Cave on Potato Creek] in the rock, situated about midway up the bluff, yawned before us.

Elated with this sudden discovery, we immediately scrambled up to explore it; found it habitable, with a spring issuing at its mouth, and encamped. It was a spacious cave, and when we had kindled our fires, the reflection of light upon its high and rugged roof, and the different apartments into which it separated, produced an effect of aweful grandeur which it is impossible to describe. The train of reflections in which we are apt to indulge is not always the effect of a previous resolution, nor is it always within the power of control; and while we partook of our frugal meal of dried venison, bread, and water, we were almost imperceptibly drawn into a conversation on the nature and objects of our journey, the hardships of the hunter's life, its advantages and disadvantages, and comparison between savage and civilized society. This carried us to other scenes, the land of our nativity, which seemed dearer in being at a distance; the conversation dropped, and we spread our skins and prepared for sleep. While the light alternately glared or faded upon the terrific walls of the cave, I engraved the date of our visit with a knife upon a smooth calcareous rock, and transcribed from my journal a part of the following inscription, previously penciled for the purpose:

> O thou, who, clothed with magical spell,
> Delight'st in lonely wilds to dwell,
> Resting in rift, or wrapt in air,
> Remote from mortal ken or care.
> Spirit of Caverns, goddess blest!
> Hear a suppliant's fond request,
> One, who nor a wanton calls
> Or intruder in thy walls;
> One, who spills not on the plain
> Blood for sport, or worldly gain,
> Like his red barbarian kin
> Deep in murder, foul in sin;
> Or with high horrific yells
> Rends thy dark and silent cells;
> But a devious traveller nigh,
> Weary, hungry, parch'd and dry:
> One who seeks thy shelter blest,
> Not to riot, but to rest,
> Grant me, from thy crystal rill,
> Oft my glittering cup to fill;
> Let thy dwelling, rude and high,
> Form our nightly canopy,
> And by super-human walls
> Ward the dew that nightly falls:
> Guard me from the ills that creep

On the houseless traveller's sleep,
From the ravenous panther's spring,
From the scorpion's poisoned sting,
From the serpent—reptile curst,
Or the Indian's midnight thrust.
Grant me sweet repose by night,
And a vision of delight!
Grant me this, and o'er my sleep
Thy aerial vigils keep.
Let me dream of friendship true,
And that human ills are few;
Let me dream that boyhood's schemes
Are not, what I've found them—dreams;
And his hopes, however gay,
Have not flitted fast away.
Let me dream life is no bubble
That the world is free of trouble,
And my heart's a stranger still
To the cares that fain would kill,
Let me dream I e'er shall find
Honour fair, or fortune kind,
And that time shall sweetly fling
In my path perpetual spring.
Let me dream my bosom never
Felt the pang from friends to sever;
And that life is not replete,
Or with loss, pain, woe, deceit,
Let me dream misfortune's smart
Ne'er hath wrung my bleeding heart,
Nor from home its potent sway
Drove me far, oh far away.
Let me dream my journey here
Is not fraught with toil severe;
That the barren is not dreary,
Nor my daily marches weary;
And the cliff, the brake, the brier,
Never wound, and never tire;
Stony couch and chilly sky,

Trackless desart, mountain dry,
These afflict not, but beguile
Time away, like beauty's smile,
Let me dream it, for I know,
When I wake, it is not so.

MONDAY, NOV. 23D.

Our horse was turned loose last night with the poorest prospect of picking up a meal than he has yet experienced, and we had our fears that the sterility of the country would induce him to stray off. In this we were not disappointed, and spent the greater part of the forenoon in looking him up. We then followed down the valley about three miles, and came to the banks of the stream we had the day before left. A considerable change in the face of the country has taken place. Instead of rich bottoms, we have a high oak-prairie. The perpendicular bluffs, and the pine, have also disappeared, and in their place we have long sloping hills, covered by oaks. The stream has also visibly increased in size, and is now deep enough to float a keel-boat of twenty tons burthen. Thinking it had received a considerable tributary from the left bank, at no great distance above, we tied our horse, and pursued up several miles, but were mistaken. On returning, we followed down about three miles, and encamped on the banks of the river. Distance ten miles. We have observed little game to-day; the weather continues pleasant.

TUESDAY, NOV. 24TH.

Got our horse packed at day-light, and travelled down the river's bank fourteen miles, and encamped. Lands chiefly poor; some bottoms of a second quality, but very narrow, and hemmed in by rocks and hills. The river has to-day, about seven miles below our encampment, received a tributary [Bryant Creek] from the right bank; and, a little below, another from the left. A singular circumstance was noticed at the former. It enters the river in a direction contrary to that of the current of the water, and with such velocity that it maintains its course for many yards up stream, until the opposing current overpowers and turns it downward.

A little below the junction of these streams we passed several Indian camps, but all in a state of decay, and bearing the appearance of having been deserted three or four years. These are the first traces of savage life (save some hacks apparently made with hatchets in saplings, noticed yesterday and to-day,) which we have seen since leaving the Fourche à Courtois. Several causes have induced the Indians to relinquish hunting in this quarter, and principally their wars among themselves, which have kept them in mutual fear of each other. Lately, the Indian title has been extinguished by purchase by the United States, and this stream will no longer be included in their hunting-grounds. It was claimed by the Osages.

The inducements for hunting are, however, great; and large quantities of bear, deer, elk, and beaver skins, might be collected. I had an opportunity this day, while travelling across a very rocky bank of the river, to observe two large and beautiful beavers who were sporting in water. They afterwards came out and sat upon a rock, occasionally changing positions, and evincing great dexterity and quickness in their movements. They were within shooting distance, but I reserved my fire a few moments to observe their motions, when suddenly they darted into their holes. The wild turkey has also been very abundant to-day, and the ducks and geese upon the river. Distance fourteen miles.

WEDNESDAY, NOV. 25TH.

The quality of the lands passed over to-day has, in general, been sterile, with little timber. A few strips of good bottom lands have intervened. In travelling ten miles, on descending the slope of a long hill, we descried at its foot a large cabin, covered with split board, and were elated with the idea of finding it inhabited by a white hunter. On coming up, however, we were disappointed. It had apparently been deserted about a year, or eighteen months. We could not, however, resist the comfortable shelter it afforded from the weather, and encamped in it at an early hour in the afternoon. The site had been chosen with the sagacity of a hunter. A stream ran in front; on the back was a thick and extensive forest; and a large cane-brake commenced near one side of it, and extended to the banks of the river, so that it afforded great facilities for procuring the three great requisites for encampment, wood, water, and horse-feed. On going to the river, we are surprised to find it considerably enlarged. It is as wide at this place as the Muskingum at Marietta, and probably affords as much water at this season of the year. The weather continues mild. Distance ten miles.

THURSDAY, NOV. 26TH.

The great width of the river, which appears to have suddenly increased, induced us to believe we were upon White River, and that the stream we have been following has discharged its waters some miles above, where the thickness of the cane and brush rendered it impossible to travel near the river's bank. To ascertain this point I went back about five miles, and took a circuit into the country on the opposite side of the river, but found our conjecture unfounded, no stream of any size coming in at that place.

It is necessary here to note, that we have for several days been in the expectation of striking the hunter settlements on White River, having already been in the woods more than double the time contemplated. Our supplies have consequently been failing for several days. Our bread gave out more than a week ago, and we have not Indian meal enough to last more than one day more. Our dried meat and our shot are also nearly expended, so that there appears a certainty of running out of provisions very soon, without the possibility of getting a supply, unless we should be fortunate enough to arrive at some hunter's cabin in the course of one or two days. We have, in fact, already been on short allowance for two days past, and begin to feel the effects of an unsatisfied appetite. The following incident will serve to show the situation to which we were reduced. In returning from the little tour of observation I made on the right banks of the river, I met with a deserted Indian, or White Hunter's Camp, where I found three pumpkins upon a vine which had sprung up from a seed accidentally dropped by the former occupant. One of them having been partly eaten by some wild animal, I gave the balance to my horse, except a portion which I reserved for my own use, and which I sat down and eat with as much pleasure as I ever enjoyed from the most delicious melon or peach. I was not, indeed, before sensible of such a degree of hunger. The other two I took to camp, where I received the hearty congratulations of my companion upon so fortunate a discovery, and arrangements were immediately made for a grand stew. A little iron camp-kettle we carried with us was well adapted for the purpose, and we had a plenty both of water and of salt; but as we had neither bread nor meat, nor any other eatable thing to make up a repast, some epicures would not have relished the entertainment. Nevertheless, we enjoyed a most hearty and social repast, for what we lacked in variety we made up in rarity; and had a haunch of venison, dressed with all the spices of the east, smoked upon our oaken table, we could not have done more ample justice to the cookery.

A circumstance has been noticed this evening, which proves that the climate we are in is adapted to the growth of cotton, several stalks of which were found growing spontaneously among the weeds encircling our camp. The bowls were handsomely filled with cotton of a fine quality, and we picked some of it, for the purpose of kindling a fire, as we find it preferable to tow, which we have heretofore used.

FRIDAY, NOV. 27TH.

Having exhausted our provisions and our shot, so that we could procure no support from our guns, we determined on leaving our heavy baggage and horse at the Hunter's Camp, in order that we might travel with greater rapidity in search of a settlement, which we had reason to believe was at no great distance. We had each provided ourselves with knapsacks, in which we put a blanket, and some other indispensables. Our horse, with a bell on, was turned into the adjacent cane-brake, and our baggage piled in one corner of the camp, secured from the weather by boards, bark, &c. With these arrangements we left the camp at an early hour, keeping on the highlands nearly parallel with the river, which ran in a general course south-south-west.

After travelling about six miles, we were rejoiced to hear a gun fired on our left, supposing it to be some hunter who could afford us relief, or at least direct us in what section of the country we were, and with this view made great exertions to find him. We fired several times; we hallooed, and were answered; but after pursuing him for some time, were obliged to give up the attempt, and pursue our way, having lost an hour or two in the search. In going eight miles further, night overtook us, and we encamped in an Indian bark tent on the bank of the river, which had not been occupied for one or two years. Distance fourteen miles. The weather is becoming cooler.

SATURDAY, NOV. 28TH.

We this morning finished the last morsel of our provisions. A dense fog, which prevented us from discerning objects at a distance of fifty yards, detained us in camp until sun-rise, when we ascended the river-hills on our left, and travelled diligently in a south-south-east course, which was that of the river, until late in the afternoon. A want of water now compelled us again to seek the river's bank, and we encamped in a thick cane-brake in season to gather up some wood, and build a fire, before dark. Our route this day has lain across a rough and sterile tract of country, covered with oak, and destitute of streams; and we have seen abundance of deer, for whom it appears to be a favourite range at this season of the year. The rocks are invariably secondary lime-stone, which has continued to be the surface rock, in all the district we have passed over, since last notice. The mineralogy has not been interesting. Iron-ores, some crystallized quartz, pyrites, and hornstone, are the principal substances noticed. The weather, which has been mild and pleasant, since we commenced our journey, has experienced a change that has gradually been operating for several days, and we have sensibly felt the increase of cold for the last two nights. The uniform temperature, 44 deg. of the air, and the serenity of the atmosphere, have been the subject of frequent remark, while we have been travelling in this section of territory. There have been a few days in which the atmosphere was smoky, but, at the same time, an increased warmth was observable; and with the exception of a slight shower of rain, which fell during the night, while encamped on the Merrimack, and a rain-storm which prevailed while in Ashley's Cave, on the Currents, the sky has remained unclouded. We did not, indeed, expect to find the climate so favourable at this season of the year, and are disposed to believe that the month of November in this region may uniformly be characterized by mild, serene, and pleasant weather. Distance fourteen miles. Acorns for supper.

Sunday, Nov. 29th.

A thick fog, which overhung the valley this morning, prevented us from quitting our camp at an early hour. When sufficiently clear to discern our way, we ascended the river-hills on our left, and took a south-south-east course across the highlands, and after travelling twelve miles, encamped in a deep ravine after dark, as we were unable before to find water. Nothing can exceed the roughness and sterility of the country we have to-day traversed; and the endless succession of steep declivities, and broken, rocky precipices, surmounted, added to a languor consequent to our situation, has rendered the day's march unusually fatiguing.

Monday, Nov. 30th.

We obtained little sleep last night on account of the cold, and commenced our journey at a very early hour this morning. After travelling two miles we fell into a horse-path with fresh tracks leading both ways, and after some deliberation followed the left-hand end of it, leading to the north-east.

There was no doubt now of our being on a path occasionally travelled between two settlements, but it was impossible to tell which of them we were nearest. We first concluded to follow to the north-east; but, on going about three miles, altered our minds, and had returned about half a mile on the same path we went, when we met a man on horseback. He was the first human being we had encountered for twenty days, and I do not know that I ever received a greater pleasure at the sight of a man. He proved to be a person who had formerly resided as a hunter at a remote settlement on White River, and was now returning from a visit to that region, where he had disposed of a small improvement. From him we learned that the stream we had been following down, was the Great North Fork of White River; that we were then within ten miles of its mouth, and that we were within a few miles of a house either way. Elated with this information, we turned about and followed our informant, who, in travelling about seven miles in a north-west direction, brought us to a hunter's house on Bennet's Bayou, a tributary stream of the North Fork, where we arrived about three o'clock in the afternoon.

Our approach was announced by the loud and long continued barking of dogs, who required repeated bidding before they could be pacified; and the first object worthy of remark which presented itself on emerging from the forest, was the innumerable quantity of deer, bear, and other skins, which had been from time to time stretched out, and hung up to dry on poles and trees around the house. These trophies of skill and prowess in the chace were regarded with great complacency by our conductor as we passed among them, and he told us, that the house we were about to visit belonged to a person by the name of Wells, who was a forehanded man for these parts, and a great hunter. He had several acres of ground in a state of cultivation, and a substantial new-built log-house, consisting of one room, which had been lately exchanged for one less calculated to accommodate a growing family. Its interior would disappoint any person who has never had an opportunity of witnessing the abode of man beyond the pale of the civilized world. Nothing could be more remote from the ideas we have attached to domestic comfort, neatness, or conveniency, without allusion to cleanliness, order, and the concomitant train of household attributes, which make up the sum of human felicity in refined society.

The dress of the children attracted our attention. The boys were clothed in a particular kind of garment made of deer-skin, which served the double

Frontier cabin. COURTESY OF THE STATE HISTORICAL SOCIETY OF MISSOURI.

purposes of shirt and jacket. The girls had buck-skin frocks, which it was evident, by the careless manner in which they were clothed, were intended to combine the utility both of linen and calico, and all were abundantly greasy and dirty. Around the walls of the room hung the horns of deer and buffaloe, rifles, shot-pouches, leather-coats, dried meat, and other articles, composing the ward-robe, smoke-house, and magazine of our host and family, while the floor displayed great evidence of his own skill in the fabri-cation of household furniture. A dressed deer-skin served up much in the shape the animal originally possessed, and filled with bear's oil, and another filled with wild honey, hanging on opposite sides of the fire-place, were too conspicuous to escape observation, for which, indeed, they appeared to be principally kept, and brought forcibly to mind the ludicrous anecdote of potatoes and point—

> "As in some Irish houses where things are so-so,
> One gammon of bacon hangs up for a show."

Our first care was to inform our host that we wished something to eat; that we had come across the wilderness from Mine à Burton, had been

twenty-four days out, and run short of shot, and that we had been without meat or bread for several days. We were about to add, that we were inexperienced in hunting and travelling in the woods, and had probably fared worse than an old hunter would have done in our situation; but he anticipated our design, notwithstanding our being disguised as hunters, and taking hold of my companion's shotgun, remarked, "I reckon, stranger, you have not been used much to travelling in the woods."

While his wife was preparing a meal, we entered into a general conversation on the subject of our journey, and obtained from him such directions as were necessary for continuing our course, which we now learned we had widely missed. He inquired respecting the country we had crossed, what were the streams, the kind of wood, and the game. All this was done with a view either of learning from us, or of judging for himself whether it was a region for hunting, and what animals it abounded with. He was particularly anxious for bear, deer being very common in all parts, and to use his own words, "hardly worth shooting;" and from information we gave him, he immediately determined to set out the next day on a bear-hunt, up the Great North Fork. His wife seemed to take a very great interest in this piece of information, and was even more particular than he in inquiries respecting the freshness of the signs we had seen.

We now sat down to a meal of smoking-hot corn-bread, butter, honey, and milk, a diet we should at any time have relished, but in the present instance very judiciously set before us; and after eating as much as we supposed two hearty men ought to, arose unsatisfied, not more from a regard to moral than physical propriety. After supper we made many inquiries respecting the region we were in; its bearing and relation to the nearest settlements; the quality of soil, mineral and vegetable productions, &c. topics upon which he readily gave us information. He was ever anxious to show that he knew something of civilized society (from which, by the way, we had afterwards reason to conclude he had made a sudden escape.) told us, that he sometimes went on business into the settled parts of Lawrence county, and that he then lived within a hundred miles of a justice of the peace, and by way of proving this, showed us a summons he had himself lately received. He desired us to read it, (a thing neither himself nor any member of his family could do,) but with all our ingenuity in deciphering syllables and connecting words, we could not tell him when, or where, the suit was to be held; who he was to answer, nor, indeed, make any sense out of it.

In the course of the evening I tried to engage our hostess and her daughters in small-talk, such as passes current in every social corner; but, for the first time, found I should not recommend myself in that way. They could only talk of bears, hunting, and the like. The rude pursuits, and the coarse enjoyments of the hunter state, were all they knew.

The evening was now far spent; we had related the most striking incidents of our tour, and had listened in return to many a hunting exploit, in the course of which, the trophies on the wall were occasionally referred to as proof, when a motion was made for sleep, and we lay down on a skin before the fire, happy in the reflection that we had a roof to cover us. Distance twelve miles.

TUESDAY, DEC. 1ST.

We had concluded to spend this day in preparations for recommencing our journey on the next. Our dress now required attention. Our shoes were literally cut to pieces by the stony region we had crossed, and we had purchased a deer-skin for the purpose of making ourselves a pair of mockasons a-piece. We also had purchased some corn for bread, some wild honey, and a little lead. The former required pounding in a mortar, and the latter moulding into bullets, or shot. All this was imperiously necessary: and we had, therefore, determined to devote the day in making preparations, but we found our host and his sons early busied in equipping themselves for a bear-hunt up the Great North Fork, and as they would pass near the place where we had left our horse and baggage on the 27th of November, determined not to lose so good an opportunity of being safely piloted back. Our wayward course for the last two days had already carried us as many miles in a direct line toward it, and he told us he could by a near route carry us there before nine o'clock at night. This served to increase our anxiety, which he had no sooner raised to the highest point, than he refused to conduct us, unless we would pay a certain sum of money, which he stipulated. He had already found we had money, for we had paid him very liberal, if not exorbitant prices, for every thing we had received, and it had only served to inflame his avarice. There was no alternative in our present situation, and we agreed to his demand, provided he would kill us a deer, either on the way, or before he left our camp. This arranged, we began early in the morning to beat our corn into meal, by means of a wooden mortar and pestle he kept for that purpose. This mortar was made by burning a hole in the top of a firm oak-stump, and a large wooden pestle attached to a spring-pole, adapted to play into it. It was an unwieldy apparatus, and worked with a tremendous clattering, attended with incredible fatigue to the operator. At eleven o'clock, however, we were ready for a march, and shouldering our knapsacks and guns, set forward toward the north-west, accompanied by our host, his sons, and a neighbour, seven men in all, armed and equipped for a bear-hunt, and followed by a troop of hungry dogs, who made the woods re-echo with their cries. They were all on horseback but ourselves, and as we were heavy laden, and sore-footed, we soon fell into the rear, which obliged the cavalcade occasionally to halt until we came up. After we had proceeded some miles, in the course of which it had been demonstrated, that we were unable to keep up with them, and that their frequent stopping would prevent our arrival at the hunter's camp that night, they offered us the privilege of riding and walking alternately with them, and with great diligence we reached the camp near ten o'clock at night, and found our horse and baggage all safe. Distance twenty miles.

WEDNESDAY, DEC. 2D.

Two men had been detached from our party yesterday for the purpose of killing the stipulated deer; and that they might proceed more cautiously, took another route, and reached the camp some time before our arrival, but were unsuccessful, only bringing in a couple of turkeys, one of which was immediately roasted for supper. Early this morning, therefore, several of the party went out in quest of game, but all returned at intervals within two hours, completely unsuccessful, and after finishing the other turkey by way of breakfast, suddenly mounted their horses and bid us adieu. So abrupt a movement took us rather by surprise, and as they trotted off through an adjoining forest, we stood surveying the singular procession, and the singular beings of whom it was composed, and which, taken altogether, bore no comparison with any thing human or divine, savage or civilized, which we had ever before witnessed, but was rather characterized in partaking of whatever was disgusting, terrific, rude, and outré in all. It was, indeed, a novel and striking spectacle, such as we had never before experienced, and when they had passed out of sight we could not forbear an expression of joy at the departure of men, in whose presence we felt rather like prisoners than associates. From their generosity we had received nothing; they had neglected to fulfill one of the most essential engagements, and departed without even an apology for it; their manner and conversation were altogether rough and obscene, and their conduct such as to make us every moment feel that we were in their power. Nothing could more illy correspond with the ideas we had formed of our reception among white hunters, than the conduct we had experienced from these men. Their avarice, their insensibility to our wants, not to call them sufferings, and their flagrant violations of engagements, has served to sink them in our estimation to a very low standard; for, deprived of its generosity, its open frankness, and hospitality, there is nothing in the hunter-character left to admire.

Left alone, we began to reflect upon our own situation, which, with every advantage that had been gained by our visit to the hunters, was still extremely unpleasant. As to provision, we had corn, meal, and some honey, but we had not enough of either to last a great while without meat; and besides, the voracious appetite created by the exertion of travelling demanded something more. We had only succeeded in procuring a sufficient quantity of lead to mould five bullets. We had purchased a skin for making mockasons. We had got directions for continuing our voyage, and knew the relative situation of the country we were in. In so much was our condition bettered, and preferable to what we found it five days before, on quitting the same camp in quest of a settlement. But we still lacked animal food, we lacked lead, and guns adapted to hunting; and we lacked that experience necessary to enable us to pursue our way successfully through a wilderness, by directions which were either very vague, or not founded on an acquaintance with that part of the country, the latter of which we had strong reasons for believing to be the case.

Our first care, after the departure of the hunters, was to make ourselves mockasons, and we spent the day in this and other preparations, necessary to the comfort, convenience, and safety of our tour.

THURSDAY, DEC. 3D.

While Mr. Pettibone completed the preparations necessary for recommencing our journey to-morrow, I sallied into the adjoining woods with my gun, with a determination to kill something. But after spending several hours in endeavouring to elude the sagacity of the birds and beasts of the forest, and making three unsuccessful shots, I returned to camp in a plight infinitely worse than I left it. Mr. P. then took the gun, and also made an unsuccessful shot at a turkey. We had now but one ball left; it was near night, and a flock of turkey betook themselves to roost on a cluster of oaks at no great distance.

As we had been unsuccessful during the day, we resolved to try our fortune at night, and endeavour to accomplish that by stratagem which we had been unable to do in any other way. The night was dark, and we presumed this animal would not be frightened from its roost by our approach. To prevent all accidents, I cleaned up my gun thoroughly, put in a new flint, and charged it with great care, with the remaining ball, having first cut it in thirty-two parts by way of shot. Then taking a torch, we proceeded into the midst of the flock, and selecting a large one, which sat low, Mr. P. fired, while I held the light above the barrel, and the turkey dropped. With joy we returned to camp, and prepared a sumptuous repast.

FRIDAY, DEC. 4TH.

The weather, which has continued mild during the whole month of November, experienced a sensible change in the last three days, and we had cold and frosty nights, and the mornings and evenings chilly. The 1st of December was a cold day, the second moderately cold, the third mild, and this day it has rained constantly, so that we have been confined to our camp.

SATURDAY, DEC. 5TH.

The weather being clear this morning, we got our horse packed at an early hour, and fording the river, pursued a west course for Sugar-Loaf Prairie, on White River. After travelling two miles across a high ridge, we struck a small river, tributary to the Great North Fork, which we followed up seven or eight miles, and encamped in a cane-brake on a low point of land, formed by the junction of two streams, near its head. Travelling had been excessively bad, owing to the hills, the roughness of the country, and the thickets along the margin of the stream. A proportion of cane-brake and swamp has also been encountered, in crossing which, our horse got mired, an accident which cost us great labour, and threatened one of the most serious calamities which has yet attended our journey. All attempts to rescue him seemed fruitless, our exertions only served to sink him deeper in the mire. We at last succeeded in getting off the pack, piece after piece, but after spending two hours in vain endeavours to extricate the horse, gave up the attempt. We now carried our baggage to a contiguous spot of dry ground, and sat down to rest, and to contemplate our own situation, which, deprived of our horse, was truly deplorable. Our skins, our cooking-utensils, axe, some part of our corn, meal, &c. must be abandoned. Without these we could not progress with any degree of comfort, and in resolving to renew our attempts, exhibited, perhaps, less of reasonable perseverance than of desperation, for, on returning to the horse, he was now sunk in soft black mud so deep, that the upper part of his back and head and neck were only visible. Nevertheless we succeeded, with less than an hour's work, in drawing him out, and cleaning the mud from his body, so that we were enabled to re-pack him, and travel on about three miles before encamping. Some tolerably good lands have been observed on the stream we came up, but generally there is a want of timber. Distance nine miles.

SUNDAY, DEC. 6TH.

Travelled sixteen miles west south west, across a rocky ridge of land, and encamped on a pretty large stream running south, from which we conclude it is discharged into White River. Face of the country very rough, lands sterile, timber oak, and very scanty; weather very mild and pleasant for the season.

MONDAY, DEC. 7TH.

On going six miles, we halted our horse near the summit of a bald mountain, while we went up to survey one of those beautiful and extensive prospects which the traveller so frequently enjoys in passing over this singularly wild and barren region. We had been told by the hunter to travel toward sun-set, that is, nearly due-west, and that in going fifteen miles we should reach a settlement of hunters on the banks of White River. We had now gone double that distance, and as we could not, from the elevated peak on which we now stood, discover any signs of White River, or of human habitations, had reason to conclude we had received wrong directions, and, therefore, resolved to alter our course of travelling. Returning to our horse, we turned directly south, making a right angle with our former course, and had not proceeded more than a mile, when we fell into a feintly-marked horse-path, and in following this three miles, it led into another and a plainer path, which led us on a high bluff of rocks, forming the eastern bank of White River, which ran a broad and beautiful stream below. Elated with this discovery, made so soon after we were ready to conclude ourselves lost, we followed down the river's bank about a mile, and discovered a house on the opposite bank of the river. We lost no time in fording it at a ripple, where the water was only half-leg deep, and were received with hospitality by the occupant, a white hunter, by the name of M'Gary. He had a field of several acres under cultivation, where he raised corn, with several horses, cows, and hogs. The house was of logs, built after the manner of the new settlers in the interior of Ohio, Indiana, and Ilinois. He was provided with a hand-mill for grinding corn, a smoke-house filled with bear and other meats, and the interior of the house, though very far from being either neat or comfortable, bore some evidence that the occupant had once resided in civilized society. I noticed a couple of odd volumes of books upon a shelf. Some part of the wearing-apparel of himself and family was of foreign manufacture. Upon the whole, he appeared to live in great ease and independence, surrounded by a numerous family of sons and daughters, all grown up; received us with cordiality, gave us plenty to eat, and bid us welcome as long as we pleased to stay.

In the evening, conversation turned on the length and object of our jour-ney, the difficulties we had encountered, the game we had seen, &c. He told us we were 800 miles above the junction of White River with the Mississippi; that the river was navigable with keel-boats all the way; that there were several settlements along its banks, the river bottoms being very rich; and that traders sometimes came up with large canoes to that place, and to the settlement above at the Sugar-Loaf Prairie. He represented our journey toward the head of the White River as extremely hazardous, on account of the Osage Indians, whose hunting grounds embraced the whole region in which this river, and its upper tributaries, originate, and who never failed to rob white hunters, and travellers who were so unfortunate as to fall in their way, and sometimes carried them into captivity. He related the par-ticulars of a robbery they had some time before committed upon him in the very house we were then sitting, when they took away horses, clothes, and such other articles about the house as they took a fancy to. They had vis-ited him in this way twice, and very recently had stolen eight beaver traps, with all his furs, from a neighbouring hunter, and detained him a consider-able time a prisoner in their camp. Numerous other instances were related, all tending to prove that the Osage Indians felt hostile to the white settle-ments along that river, and that they were habitual robbers and plunderers, not only of them, but of every person who happened to fall defenceless into their hands.

All this was new to us, and excited some surprise, as the United States have enjoyed an uninterrupted peace with this tribe of Indians ever since the acquisition of Louisiana. We replied to him, that the existence of such robberies must certainly be unknown to the government; that we considered it bound to protect them in the lawful and peaceable enjoyment of their liberty and property while living within the territories of the United States, and that if proper representations were made to the Indian agent at St. Louis, redress could undoubtedly be obtained. He said such representations had been attempted, but owing to causes not recollected, did not succeed; that they were not, in fact, able to undertake such long journeys for the purpose of seeking redress, which would cost more than the worth of the property taken, &c.

IIe also informed us, that a deadly and deep-rooted hostility existed between the Cherokees, who had lately exchanged their lands in Tennessee for the country lying between the Arkansaw and Red River, and the Osages, and that they were daily committing depredations upon the territories and properties of each other. Having but a short time before witnessed the conclusion of a treaty of peace between these two tribes, made at St. Louis under the auspices of Governor Clark, I was surprised to hear of the continuance of hostilities. To prove what reliance is to be placed on the faith of such treaties, he mentioned, that when the Cherokees returned from the council which concluded that treaty, they pursued a party of Osages near the banks of White River, and stole, unperceived, twenty horses, and carried them safely off. Before going to sleep we determined to leave our horse, who had fallen away very much, and indeed all our baggage which cannot be put into knapsacks, with M'Gary, until our return. Distance eleven miles.

TUESDAY, DEC. 8TH.

Having obtained the necessary information, we determined this morning to continue our journey to Sugar-Loaf Prairie, for which we had made preparation, by turning a couple of small bags into knapsacks, and putting in a blanket, and such articles of necessity as could be conveniently carried. On offering to pay our entertainer for victuals and lodging, he refused to take any thing, and perceiving we had no meat to take with us, took me to his smoke-house, and drawing his knife, put it into my hand, then opened the door, and told me to go in and cut what I wanted. I did so. It was well filled with dried buffaloe's beef, and bear's meat, both smoked and fresh. At nine o'clock in the morning we bid our generous host adieu, crossed the river at the ford, and followed up the horse-path leading to Sugar-Loaf Prairie, on the east bank of the river. This path frequently became so blind, that we were unable to keep it, and spent some time in frequent searches for the tracks of horses. Relieved of the tiresome task of leading a pack-horse, we travelled on with accelerated speed, until approaching darkness warned us that it was time to encamp. Deer and Turkey have been common. The weather continues mild. Distance sixteen miles. Course west-north-west.

WEDNESDAY, DEC. 9TH.

The path we are pursuing became so feint and indefinite, that we were unable to follow it more than a mile from our encampment, but taking the general course of the river, forced our way through the thick cane and brier which over-run the rich alluvial banks of the river, with incredible fatigue. At the distance of seven miles we came unexpectedly into a small opening in the midst of one of the most gloomy thickets of cane we had yet encountered. Here, in a small camp, tight only at top, we found a family who had two weeks before emigrated from the lower parts of White River. They had brought their furniture and effects, such as it was, partly in a canoe up the river, and partly on pack-horses through the woods.

Nothing could present a more striking picture of the hardships encountered by the back wood's settler, than this poor, friendless, and forlorn family. The woman and her little children were a touching groupe of human distress, and in contemplating their forlorn situation we for a while forgot our own deprivations and fatigues. They were short of provisions, the husband being out in search of game, and after obtaining such information as the woman was able to give, respecting the next settlement, we continued our journey in a north-west course along the hills which skirt the river bottoms at the distance of a mile from its banks, and arrived at an early hour in the afternoon at the house of a Mr. Coker, at what is called Sugar-Loaf Prairie. This takes its name from a bald hill covered with grass rising on the verge of the river alluvion on the west side of the river, and is discernible at the distance of many miles. The settlement at Sugar-Loaf Prairie consists at present of four families, located within the distance of eight miles, but is so recent that a horse-path has not yet been worn from one cabin to another. It is the highest settlement on the river, excepting two families at the mouth of Beaver Creek, about three miles above [the actual distance is fifteen miles overland and forty miles by river]. These people subsist partly by agricul-

Sugarloaf Knob and Sugarloaf Prairie northeast of Lead Hill, Arkansas, 1994.
PHOTOGRAPH BY MILTON RAFFERTY.

ture, and partly by hunting. They raise corn for bread, and for feeding their horses previous to the commencement of long journeys in the woods, but none for exportation. No cabbages, beets, onions, potatoes, turnips, or other garden vegetables, are raised. Gardens are unknown. Corn and wild meats, chiefly bear's meat, are the staple articles of food. In manners, morals, customs, dress, contempt of labour and hospitality, the state of society is not essentially different from that which exists among the savages. Schools, religion, and learning are alike unknown. Hunting is the principal, the most honourable, and the most profitable employment. To excel in the chace procures fame, and a man's reputation is measured by his skill as a marksman, his agility and strength, his boldness and dexterity in killing game, and his patient endurance and contempt of the hardships of the hunter's life. They are, consequently, a hardy, brave, independent people, rude in appearance, frank and generous, travel without baggage, and can subsist any where in the woods, and would form the most efficient military corps in frontier warfare which can possibly exist. Ready trained, they require no discipline, inured to danger, and perfect in the use of the rifle. Their system of life is, in fact, one continued scene of camp-service. Their habitations are not always permanent, having little which is valuable, or loved, to rivet their affections to any one spot; and nothing which is venerated, but what they can carry with them; they frequently change residence, travelling where game is more abundant. Vast quantities of beaver, otter, raccoon, deer, and bear-skins, are annually caught. These skins are carefully collected and preserved during the summer and fall, and taken down the river in canoes, to the mouth of the Great North Fork of White River, or to the mouth of Black River, where traders regularly come up with large boats to receive them. They also take down some wild honey, bear's bacon, and buffaloe-beef, and receive in return, salt, iron-pots, axes, blankets, knives, rifles, and other articles of first importance in their mode of life.

We were received by Mr. Coker with that frankness and blunt hospitality which are characteristic of the hunter. Our approach to the house was, as usual, announced by the barking of dogs, whose incessant yells plainly told us, that all who approached that domain, of which they were the natural guardians, and whether moving upon two, or upon four legs, were considered as enemies, and it was not until they were peremptorily, and repeatedly recalled, that they could be pacified. Dried skins, stretched out with small rods, and hung up to dry on trees and poles around the house, served to give the scene the most novel appearance. This custom has been observed at every hunter's cabin we have encountered, and, as we find, great pride is taken in the display, the number and size of the bear-skins serving as a credential of the hunter's skill and prowess in the chace.

We had no sooner acquainted our entertainer with the objects and contemplated extent of our journey, than he discovered the fear which appears to prevail on this river, respecting the Osage Indians, and corroborated what we had before heard of their robberies. He considered the journey hazardous at this season, as they had not yet, probably, broke up their hunting camps, and retired, as they do every winter, to their villages on the Grandosaw (Grand Osage) river. He recommended us to abandon our guns for rifles, to take with us as little baggage as possible—thought we should find it a poor season for game, and made other remarks of a discouraging nature. The fact was, he had an old rifle for sale, thought we had money, and wished to get double the worth of it, and wished us to engage an idle hypochondriac, who hung about him, as a guide. We were inclined to do both, but could not agree as to the price of the former, and the latter could not be prevailed to go at any price.

THURSDAY, DEC. 10TH.

On first striking White River, at M'Gary's, we endeavoured to procure a guide to conduct us on our route, but were unsuccessful; being disappointed in our application here also, we took directions for reaching the hunters' camps at Beaver Creek, and left Coker's about noon. He refused taking pay for our entertainment. After travelling eight miles in a north-west course, which carried us across a hilly barren tract, extending eastwardly from the river, we encamped before dark, under a ledge of shelving lime-stone rock, the atmosphere portending a storm.

The weather begins to assume a wintery character; this is the first day we have been troubled with cold fingers.

FRIDAY, DEC. 11TH.

A singular species of deception has occurred to us in the course of this day's journey. We had been told, that in travelling a due north-west course for eighteen miles, we should strike Beaver Creek, which we were to pursue down to its mouth, where a couple of hunters had located themselves. We had, however, deviated too far to the west, and arrived at about two o'clock on the banks of White River, which we mistook for Beaver Creek, and fording it, at waist deep, pursued our course about two miles beyond, when we became sensible of the error, turned back, and pursued up on the west bank of the river until evening. We now found ourselves on a gravelly barren point of land, encompassed on both sides by water, without wood, and exposed to a keen air blowing down the river. The day-light had already disappeared; on the west bank was a high bluff of lime-stone rock rising perpendicularly from the water's edge, and so precipitous that it could not be passed; on the east was an extensive bottom of rich alluvion land, covered by forest-trees and cane, and separated from us by the main channel of the river. The very idea of wading through it, at this late hour, and cold as we were, made us shiver, yet we could not long hesitate between remaining without a stick of wood to kindle a fire, and fording the river, at this place 300 yards in width, with a depth of from four to five feet. On gaining the opposite shore, we were so chilled, that it was with difficulty a fire could be raised, and I confess this to have been one of the most cheerless nights we experienced on our tour. Distance sixteen miles, weather windy and cold.

SATURDAY, DEC. 12TH.

The ground this morning was covered with a thick white frost, the air keen and cold, and having been prevented from getting much sleep during the night by the severity of the weather, we left our encampment at day-break, and ascended the bluff, bordering the river bottom at the distance of a mile on the east.

In travelling a few miles we observed a smoke issuing from the ground, in a column about two feet in diameter, as if produced by subterranean fire. On coming up, however, it proved to be a warm dense air escaping from a cavern [probably Cathedral Cave] below, through a small aperture in the rock. All was dark within, but by throwing down stones, it appeared evident from the noise, that there was a large cavity, and thinking it might repay the risk and trouble of going down, I determined to descend; or, at least, to make the attempt. There was just room enough at the mouth to squeeze myself in, and I supported myself against the rocks, carefully feeling my way down, and as I descended, could see the light from above. At the distance of twenty feet, this orifice, which had increased gradually, though irregularly, in size, opened into a spacious chamber, terrific in appearance from its rugged walls, viewed by the feeble light transmitted from above. In three several directions, passages of nearly equal size diverged, as from a centre, descending gradually into the earth, and appearing like rents caused by some mighty convulsion. I followed down one of these as far as the least glimmering of light could be discerned, and groped along some distance further, but as this was rather a dangerous business, and I had no light for exploring with any degree of satisfaction, I gave up the attempt, bringing out a fragment of the rock, which appeared, on inspection, to be similar in every respect to the rock on the surface, viz. secondary lime-stone.

Following the course of the river, which is devious beyond comparison, we found ourselves at the distance of about six miles on the banks of Beaver Creek, a beautiful, clear stream of sixty yards wide, with an average depth of about two feet, and a handsome gravelly bottom. A little beyond this we found a horse-path, which led, within the distance of a mile and a half, to the hunters' camps we were in search of. Distance eleven miles.

III

Delayed at the Beaver Creek Settlement

SUNDAY, DEC. 13TH.

We are now at the last hunter-settlement on the river, which is, also, the most remote bound to which the white hunter has penetrated in a south-west direction from the Mississippi river, toward the rocky mountains. It consists of two families, Holt and Fisher by name, who have located themselves here within the last four months. They have not yet cleared any land for corn, nor finished their houses, notwithstanding the advanced season. They have fixed the site of their habitations on the east banks of the river, on the verge of a very large and rich tract of bottom land, occupying a bend in the river. It is covered by a heavy forest of oak, ash, maple, walnut, mulberry, and sycamore, the latter skirting the immediate banks of the river, with a vigorous growth of cane below. The opposite bank of the river is a perpendicular bluff of lime-stone rock, rising at the water's edge to a height of 300 feet, where it terminates in very rugged peaks, capped by a stinted growth of cedars and oaks, and forming a most striking contrast with the level, rich, and heavy wooded plain below, over which it casts its broad shadow by half-past three in the afternoon, which must render it a cool and delightful residence in summer. The bold and imposing effect of this scene is much heightened by beholding two natural pyramids, or towers of rock, ascending with a surprising regularity from the highest wall of the bluff, to a height of fifty or sixty feet, while all the surrounding stratum of rock has submitted during the lapse of ages to the powerful force of attrition, and been carried by rains, and by gravitation, into the adjoining vallies, whence, being comminuted by the action of water, it has been discharged through the Mississippi into the ocean. Without referring the origin of these remarkable pillars of stone to such, or similar causes, it is impossible to reconcile their appearance with the general aspect and economy of mineral nature.

Our first care on reaching this spot, was to endeavour to procure one of the hunters to guide us on our way, but in this we have not, as yet, been successful. They are strongly impressed with a fear of being robbed by the Osage Indians, and represent that they have not corn enough to last their families until our return; that their camps are not yet finished, &c.

MONDAY, DEC. 14TH.

The love of gain, which so strongly characterizes polished society in all parts of the world, has also found its way into these remote woods. We have travelled over many a trackless desart, and uninhabited plain. We have crossed that boundary in our lands, within which virtue prompts, wisdom teaches, and law restrains; we are beyond the pale of civilized society, with all its endearments, inquietudes, and attractions; but we are not beyond the influence of money, which is not confined by geographical boundaries, or located in its operation upon any particular class of society, or degree of civilization. We, accordingly, found this, after all their plausible excuses, the only real obstacle in the way of our agreement with them to accompany us as guides, but thought it advisable to submit to a little imposition, in order to accomplish our main design in visiting this region, and have just concluded a bargain with Holt. He is to have our horse, and ten dollars, to accompany us as guide and hunter, with the benefit of all skins or furs he may collect on the tour. He is first to go about 100 miles down the river, to purchase corn from some wealthy hunters there, for the use of his family. In the meantime we shall remain, and employ ourselves in making a canoe to descend the river on our return, or in completing the hunters' cabins, so that they may leave their families in a comfortable situation while we are absent. Fisher concludes to accompany us gratuitously, but would not go unless Holt went as guide, from which it is evident they have a perfect understanding of each other's views.

TUESDAY, DEC. 15TH.

The hunters did not get ready to start on their preliminary tour after corn in season to set out before noon, and determined to defer starting until to-morrow. In the afternoon we assisted them in splitting boards, and covering the roof of a log-house. The weather continues cold.

WEDNESDAY, DEC. 16TH.

This morning Holt and Fisher, accompanied by a son of the latter, with three horses, set out on a journey to purchase corn, which they intend carrying on their horses, in a particular kind of narrow leathern bag, kept for that purpose. We have been employed in chopping wood for the use of the family, as we are left, *ad interim,* to protect and provide for the women and children. The weather is now severely cold. There has, this day, for the first, been floating ice in the river, and water freezes in a few moments in the cabin.

THURSDAY, DEC. 17TH.

Employed in chopping wood, and clearing land. Our day's work, during the hunters' absence, will be much the same, and made up chiefly of the following particulars: in the morning, rise at, or before day-break, and build a large cabin-fire, of logs eight feet long; then pound the corn which is to serve the family during the day. This is done in a wooden mortar, with a pestle attached to a spring pole. The time from this to breakfast is employed in patching mockasons, &c. We then sally out into the forest with our axes, and chop and clear away cane and brush until dinner, which answers also for supper, and happens about five o'clock, so that we never sit down without an appetite. Our bill of fare presents no variety. We have homony, that is, corn boiled until it is soft, and bear's bacon for dinner, without any vegetables. The same for breakfast, with the addition of sassafras-tea. The day's work closes with building a large night-fire, and packing up, from the adjoining forest, wood enough to replenish it during the night, and succeeding day. We then lie down on a bear-skin before the fire, and enjoy the sweet repose resulting from daily labour. The weather continues cold and frosty. Water poured upon the corn this morning previous to pounding, froze in carrying it from the cabin to the mortar, a distance of thirty yards.

FRIDAY, DEC. 18TH.

Employed as yesterday. We are sometimes led to contrast the force of habit on different persons, or different classes of society; but it is only on comparing the manners and customs of people widely separated, and whose modes of life and of thinking are wholly dissimilar from our own, that the power of moral or physical habit is rendered striking, or extraordinary. We have had frequent occasion, while sojourning among the hunters in this region, to draw such comparisons. A few instances may here be mentioned. We had furnished our travelling pack with a quantity of choice young hyson-tea, and this morning made a pot of it, and invited Mrs. Fisher to partake, presuming it would be highly relished, but were surprised to hear her declare it was bitter, and unpalatable stuff. She could not drink it. She preferred dittany, sassafras, and spice-wood tea, to our hyson. We had not before imagined that there was any part of the white population of the Untied States strangers to this plant, so universally in use in our country.

Some days ago, a young child of Mrs. H being taken violently ill with what I considered a bilious attack, I administrated one of "Lee's pills," which gave effectual relief, and the child suddenly recovered. This incident served to give them great confidence in my skill, and led to further applications. Mrs. F., whose delicate situation was apparent, had she not mentioned it, feared the consequences of a costive habit, and applied to me for relief. Having little experience in these matters, I felt great delicacy and reluctance in giving any advice, but ventured on recommending a few of my anti-bilious pills, which had the desired effect. One of her daughters, a girl of fourteen, now applied; in short, before I left their cabins, I dealt out all my pills, and acquired the reputation of being a great doctor.

Justice, which in civilized society is administered through all the formalities of the law, is here obtained in a more summary way. Two hunters having a dispute respecting a horse, which one had been instrumental in stealing from the other, the person aggrieved meeting the other, some days afterwards, in the woods, shot him through the body. He immediately fled, keeping in the woods for several weeks, when the neighbouring hunters, aroused by so glaring an outrage, assembled and set out in quest of him. Being an expert woodman, he eluded them for some time, but at last they got a glimpse of him as he passed through a thicket, and one of the party fired upon him. The ball passed through his shoulder, but did not kill him. This event happened a few days before our arrival, but I know not how it has terminated. In all probability several lives will be lost before a pacification takes place, as both parties have their friends, and all are hot for revenge.

SATURDAY, DEC. 19TH.

Engaged in chopping until noon. In the afternoon we crossed the river on the ice, and visited the pyramidal rocks before mentioned. The west bank of the river, at this place, consists of a rugged wall of lime-stone, on the top of which the two pyramids are situated. The ascent to them lies through a deep defile of rocks, through which we passed with great difficulty, climbing up by the roots of the cedar, and rugged projections of rock, and occasionally leaping from one overhanging promontory to another—

> "O'er toppling rocks, where stinted briers grow,
> Cautiously, fearfully, tremblingly we go:
> Passing by devious path, and dreadful steep,
> Where the black serpent takes his sunny sleep,
> And one mistaken tread, or whirling brain,
> Is fraught with instant death, or lingering pain."   MS.

In crossing over the river, the remarkable purity of the water attracted our attention, producing a deception similar to that experienced on the 21st of November, in fording the Great North Fork of White River, the depth of the water, which appears to be only five or six feet, being in reality, more than twenty. The ice, too, is so clear, that, in walking across, it appeared as if we were walking on a pane of glass, reflecting every inequality of bottom, pebble, &c. with as much accuracy in this depth, as if covered by a pane of glass in a merchant's case.

SUNDAY, DEC. 20TH.

Observed as a day of rest. The weather this day has been perceptibly milder, and a little smoky.

MONDAY, DEC. 21ST.

Employed until three o'clock in splitting and hewing planks for a floor to Holt's cabin, when rain compelled us to quit.

TUESDAY, DEC. 22D.

The rain ceased this morning, leaving the atmosphere foggy, damp, and warm. Employed in completing the job commenced yesterday.

WEDNESDAY, DEC. 23D.

About ten o'clock this morning, Holt and Fisher returned, laden with corn. The day has been mild and pleasant, the dense fog having entirely disappeared, giving place to a clear blue sky.

THURSDAY, DEC. 24TH.

Employed in hewing out a table, daubing and chinking the house, &c. We this day left Fisher's, and removed to Holt's, a distance of half-a-mile, having now got his cabin in a comfortable condition. The hunter, although habitually lazy, and holding in contempt the pursuits of agriculture, so far, at least, as is not necessary to his own subsistence, is nevertheless a slave to his dog, the only object around him to which he appears really devoted. His horse, cow, and hogs, if he have any, living upon vegetable food, can subsist themselves in the woods; but the dog requires animal food, which he cannot himself alone procure, and to furnish which occupies no inconsiderable portion of the hunter's time. It is no easy task to provide a pack of hungry dogs, from six to twelve, the usual number owned by every hunter, with meat, the truth of which we have witnessed for several days past, and the hunters went out this morning to kill meat enough to supply them until our return. They had several days before killed a buffaloe, a bear, and a panther, about twelve miles above, on the banks of the river, but not having their horses with them, concealed it in the woods in such a way as to prevent its being devoured by the wolves. They embarked early this morning in a canoe to bring it in, and returned in the afternoon with the bear, and a part of the buffaloe, the wolves having, notwithstanding its being scaffolded, got up, and destroyed the rest. They also brought down some of the leg-bones of the buffaloe for the sake of the marrow they contain, which they told us is considered a great delicacy, intending it as a treat to us. These bones are boiled in water to cook the marrow and then cracked with an axe, and the marrow taken out. The quantity is immense. It is eaten while hot, with salt, and with the appetites we now possess, and which are voracious, we have eaten it with a high relish. A very high value is set upon a good dog by the hunter, and they are sought with the greatest avidity. We have been told of a hunter, who lately exchanged a cow for a dog, but this is considered extraordinary even here.

Friday, Dec. 25th.

Christmas-day. Employed in splitting oak-boards, &c. At our suggestion, the hunters went out to kill some turkeys, as we wished one for a Christmas-dinner, and after an absence of a couple of hours, returned with fourteen. I prevailed on Mrs. H. to undertake a turkey-pie with Indian meal crust, which we partook of under a shady tree on the banks of the river, the weather being warm and pleasant.

Saturday, Dec. 26th.

Employed in beating meal for bread on our tour. We have, at last, obviated every difficulty opposing our progress, and got matters in readiness for continuing our journey, to-morrow being fixed upon for starting, should the weather prove favourable.

Sunday, Dec. 27th.

Rain, which began last night, prevented our starting this day, which has been improved in reflection and rest. The sabbath is not known by any cessation of the usual avocations of the hunter in this region. To him all days are equally unhallowed, and the first and the last day of the week find him alike sunk in unconcerned sloth, and stupid ignorance. He neither thinks for himself, not reads the thoughts of others, and if he ever acknowledges his dependence upon the Supreme Being, it must be in that silent awe produced by the furious tempest, when the earth trembles with concussive thunders, and lightning shatters the oaks around his cottage, that cottage which certainly never echoed the voice of human prayer. In conversation a few days ago, with our host, on the subject of religion, he observed that when living on the banks of the Mississippi, some years ago, he occasionally attended a methodist-meeting and thought it a very good thing, but had found as many rogues there as any where else, and on account of a particular act of dishonesty in one of the members of the church, had determined never to go again, and had since thought there was no great use in religion; that a man might be as good without going to church as with it, and that it seemed to him to be a useless expense to be paying preachers for telling us a string of falsehoods, &c. He said, that itinerant preachers sometimes visited the lower parts of White River, and had penetrated within 300 miles of the place where we then sat, but had not found much encouragement.

Schools are also unknown, and no species of learning cultivated. Children are wholly ignorant of the knowledge of books, and have not learned even the rudiments of their own tongue. Thus situated, without moral restraint, brought up in the uncontrolled indulgence of every passion and without a regard of religion, the state of society among the rising generation in this region is truly deplorable. In their childish disputes, boys frequently stab each other with knives, two instances of which have occurred since our residence here. No correction was administered in either case, the act being rather looked upon as a promising trait of character. They begin to assert their independence as soon as they can walk, and by the time they reach the age of fourteen, have completely learned the use of the rifle, the arts of trapping beaver and otter, killing the bear, deer, and buffalo, and dressing skins and making mockasons and leather clothes. They are then accomplished in all customary things, and are, therefore, capable of supporting themselves and a family, and accordingly enter into marriage early in life. The women are observed to have few children, and of those, being deprived of the benefit of medical aid, an unusual number die in their infancy. This is probably owing wholly to adventitious causes, and may be explained on the same principles as a similar circumstance in savage life, the female being frequently exposed to the inclemency of the weather, always to unusual hardships and fatigues, doing in many instances the man's work, living in camps on the wet ground, without shoes, &c. Mrs. H. tells me, she has not lived in a cabin which had a floor to it for several years; that during that time they have changed their abode several times, and that she has lost four children, who all died before they reached their second year. The girls are brought up with little care, and inured to servile employments. They have ruddy complexions, but, in other respects, are rather gross, as they live chiefly on animal food. Being deprived of all the advantages of dress, possessed by our fair country-women in the east, they are by no means calculated to inspire admiration, but on the contrary disgust; their whole wardrobe, until the age of twelve, consisting of one greasy buckskin frock, which is renewed whenever worn out.

Among all classes superstition is prevalent. Witchcraft, and a belief in the sovereign virtue of certain metals, so prevalent in those periods of the history of the progress of the human mind, which reflect disgrace upon our species, have still their advocates here. Mr. F. related to us an amusing story of a rifle he had, that was bewitched, so that he could kill nothing with it, and sold it on that account. He had fixed his suspicions upon a neighbour, and was full in belief that he had, out of malice, laid a spell upon his rifle.

Mrs. H. had a brass ring which she had worn for several years, and declared it to be an infallible remedy for the cramp, which she was much troubled with before putting on the ring, but had not had the slightest return of it since. She was now in much distress, on account of having lately broken it so that it could not be worn, and observing that I collected ores and minerals, thought I might possess some skill in working metals, and solicited me to mend it. It was in vain I represented it was not the case; that I had no blow-pipe, or other necessary apparatus for that purpose; she was convinced I could do it, and I did not wish to show a disobliging disposition by refusing to make the attempt. By cutting several small stems of cane of different thicknesses, and fitting one into the other until the aperture was drawn down to the required degree of fineness, I soon made a blow-pipe. A hollow cut in a billet of wood, and filled with live hickory coals, answered instead of a lamp; and with a small bit of silver, and a little borax applied to the ring, and submitted to the influence of my wooden blow-pipe, I soon soldered the ring, and afterwards filed off the redundant silver with a file that happened to be among the moveable property of our host. When I made Mrs. H. a table out of the butt of an enormous white ash-log, she declared I must be a carpenter; when I relieved her child from a bilious attack, she was inclined to consider me a physician; but she was now convinced I was a silversmith.

IV

The Tour to the Lead Mines on the James River

MONDAY, DEC. 28TH.

This morning we commenced our journey towards the north, accompanied by Holt and Fisher, both on horseback, and provided with rifles. Holt goes as guide, being acquainted with the regions we are about to visit, and both are expert hunters, so that we are neither under apprehensions of losing our way, or suffering for want of provisions. The weather is chilly and unsettled. Travelled ten miles, and encamped in a valley at dusk. Killed one deer.

TUESDAY, DEC. 29TH.

The country passed over yesterday, after leaving the valley of White River, presented a character of unvaried sterility, consisting of a succession of limestone ridges, skirted with a feeble growth of oaks, with no depth of soil, often bare rocks upon the surface, and covered with coarse wild grass; and sometimes we crossed patches of ground of considerable extent, without trees or brush of any kind, and resembling the Illinois prairies in appearance, but lacking their fertility and extent. Frequently these prairies occupied the tops of conical hills, or extended ridges, while the intervening valleys were covered with oaks, giving the face of the country a very novel aspect, and resembling, when viewed in perspective, enormous sand-hills promiscuously piled up by the winds. At the foot of one of the highest and most remarkable of these, called the Bald-hill [probably Helphrey Hill], and known among hunters who travel in this quarter as a land-mark, we last night

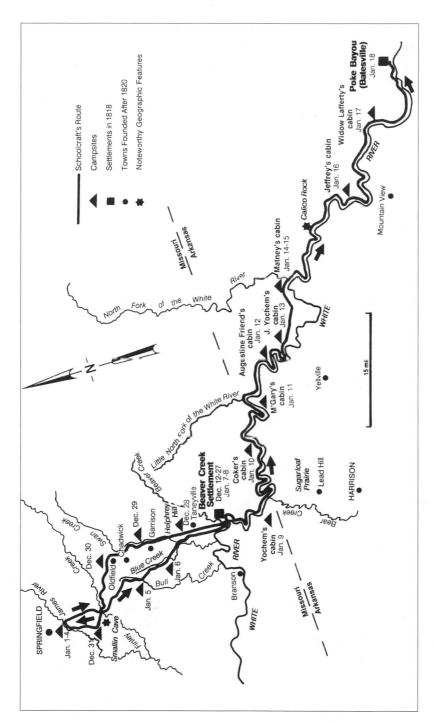

Tour route from the Beaver Creek settlement to the lead mine on James River and on to Poke Bayou. CARTOGRAPHY BY HEATHER CONLEY.

encamped. No alteration was observed in the aspect of the country, this morning, for the first six miles, when we descended into the valley of Swan Creek, a clear stream of thirty yards wide, which joins the main current of White River, about forty miles below. Its banks afford a strip of rich alluvial bottom, covered with a heavy growth of maple, hickory, ash, hackberry, elm, and sycamore, and its waters are frequented by the beaver. In following up this stream about five miles it commenced raining, and we were compelled to encamp, sheltering ourselves in some degree under the broad knots of fallen trees and limbs. Distance ten miles.

WEDNESDAY, DEC. 30TH.

In pursuing up the valley of Swan Creek, about nine miles, we fell into the Osage trace, a horse-path beaten by the Osages in their hunting excursions along this river, and passed successively three of their camps, now deserted, all very large, arranged with much order and neatness, and capable of quartering probably 100 men each. Both the method of building camps, and the order of encampment observed by this singular nation of savages, are different from anything of the kind I have noticed among the various tribes of aboriginal Americans, through whose territories I have had occasion to travel. The form of the tent or camp may be compared to an inverted bird's nest, or hemisphere, with a small aperture left in the top, for the escape of smoke; and a similar, but larger one, at one side, for passing in and out. It is formed by cutting a number of slender flexible green-poles of equal length, sharpened at each end, stuck in the ground like a bow, and, crossing at right angles at the top, the points of entrance into the ground forming a circle. Small twigs are then wove in, mixed with the leaves of cane, moss, and grass, until it is perfectly tight and warm. These tents are arranged in large circles, one within another, according to the number of men intended to be accommodated. In the centre is a scaffolding for meat, from which all are supplied every morning, under the inspection of a chief, whose tent is conspicuously situated at the head of the encampment, and differs from all the rest, resembling a half cylinder inverted. Their women and children generally accompany them on these excursions, which often occupy three months. The boys and lazy drones who do not help in hunting, are obliged to eat the intestines of the animals killed. The white hunter, on encamping in his journeys, cuts down green-trees, and builds a large fire of long logs, sitting at some distance from it. The Indian hunts up a few dry limbs, cracks them into little pieces a foot in length, builds a small fire, and sits close by it. He gets as much warmth as the white hunter, without half the labour, and does not burn more than a fiftieth part of the wood. The Indian considers the forest his own, and is careful in using and preserving every thing which it affords. He never kills more meat than he has occasion for. The white hunter destroys all before him, and cannot resist the opportunity of killing game, although he neither wants the meat, nor can carry the skins. I was particularly struck with an instance of this wanton practice, which lately occurred on White River. A hunter returning from the woods heavy laden with the flesh and skins of five bears, unexpectedly arrived in the midst of a drove of buffalo, and wantonly shot down three, having no other object than the sport of killing them. This is one of the causes of the enmity existing between the white and the red hunters of Missouri. On reaching the third Osage encampment, we left the valley of Swan Creek, holding a north-west course, and immediately entered on a high, sterile ridge of land, which separates the waters of Swan Creek from Findley's River [Finley Creek]. Finding no water at the proper time for stopping, we travelled two hours after dark, and encamped in a barren little valley without wood. Distance twenty miles.

THURSDAY, DEC. 31ST.

Within a mile after quitting the spot of our encampment, we entered the valley of Findley's Fork, or river, a large stream running from the north-east, and tributary to James' river [James River], the main north-western branch of White River. We pursued down this stream five miles, passing over a body of well-wooded, fertile river bottom, when the severity of the weather induced us to stop and build a fire to warm ourselves. This stream has been named by the hunters in allusion to the first white beaver trapper who ventured to set his traps in its waters, and the beaver is still found in it. We now quit the river, ascending the highlands which divide it from James' River, and encamped at an early hour on the banks of a small stream, in a well-wooded and fertile country. Distance twelve miles. Course north-west. Killed one deer, two turkeys, one wolf, and one wild-goose.

FRIDAY, JAN. 1ST

On leaving Findley's Fork, we followed up a small deep valley, which in a short distance, and after a few windings, terminated suddenly in a cave opening [Smallin Cave] on a hill-side the whole width of the valley, with a stream running from its mouth. The first appearance of this stupendous cavern struck us with astonishment, succeeded by a curiosity to explore its hidden recesses. Its width across, at the mouth, could not be estimated at less than 200 feet, with a height of about ninety or 100 at the highest point, descending each way, and forming, when viewed in front, a semi-circle, indented alternately, with projecting and retreating rocks. It keeps this size for several hundred feet, when a gradual diminution takes place, which continues until it is not more than ten feet across, where our progress was stopped by the stream of water which occupies the whole width of the passage, and the water, being dammed up below by a stalactitic incrustation deposited from it, forms a small lake in the bottom of the cave. Its depth appears in some places ten or fifteen feet, and the singular calcareous formation by which it is encompassed, gives it the appearance of a stupendous vase, or bath. The outlet of this natural bath presents, at a depression of ten feet below, another, but smaller lake, encompassed by a similar deposition of calcareous matter, hardened by the absorption of carbonic acid gas from the atmosphere. Large masses of stalagmite, and several columns of stalactite, pendant from the roof, are also found; but the percolation of water, to whose agency the formation of these substances are generally referred, has entirely ceased.

In that part of the cave which is dry, and in the bottom of the brook which runs across it, is found a singular calcareous formation, in the shape of small globules from the size of a grain of sand to that of a musket-bullet, which covers the bottom of the cave to the depth of a foot or more, so that in walking upon it the foot sinks, as if on a bank of loose dry sand. Some appearances of salt-petre are also furnished in crevices of the rock, which is secondary lime-stone; and, upon the whole, the cave, from its extent, which remains unknown, and the number and variety of curious and interesting objects it presents, is well worthy of a day's attention. To explore it, a boat would be necessary. We spent but an hour in it, the hunters being satisfied after gazing a few minutes, and anxious to continue the journey.

On quitting the cave, we entered on a district of country characterized by gentle sloping hills, well wooded with oak and hickory, with some extensive prairies, and a pretty fertile black soil, and encamped last night on the banks of a small stream, affording some handsome sites for plantations. On travelling two miles this morning we entered a rich and extensive valley, and found ourselves unexpectedly on the banks of James' River, the stream we were in search of. It is the principal north western fork of White River, and a large, clear, and beautiful stream. It originates in high-lands, a little south of the Gasconade river, which falls into the Missouri above St. Charles, and

Smallin Cave, 1995. PHOTOGRAPH BY MILTON RAFFERTY.

running in an opposite direction for two hundred and fifty miles, forms a junction with the south fork of White River, one hundred miles below. Along its banks are found extensive bodies of the choicest land, covered by a large growth of forest-trees and cane, and interspersed with prairies. Oak, maple, white and black walnut, elm, mulberry, hackberry, and sycamore, are the common trees, and attain a very large size. On the west commences a prairie of unexplored extent, stretching off towards the Osage river, and covered with tall rank grass. Towards its mouth, it is said to be bordered with high rocky bluffs. We forded the river on horseback, and pursuing up its western bank about four miles, encamped near the shore, in the vicinity of a lead-mine. Distance six miles. Weather cold and piercing. Killed one prairie-hen and one goose.

SATURDAY, JAN. 2D.

Calculating to remain here several days previous to our return, we spent the afternoon of yesterday in constructing a comfortable camp, and covering the roof with bark, &c. This morning, at day-light, it commenced snowing, but ceased about eight o'clock, and continued clear, with the exception of occasional flickerings, until two o'clock, when a snow-storm set in, which continued till night, and confined us to our camp. In the interim, we went out to examine the lead-mine, which is situated in the west bank, and in the bottom of the river, as lumps of ore can be seen through the water, which is very clear and transparent. The ore is galena, or sulphuret of lead, accompanied by sulphuret of zinc, and imbedded in the bank of the river in a red clay. The bottom of the river is a rock of secondary lime-stone, stratified. Killed six turkeys and one wolf.

SUNDAY, JAN. 3D.

The snow ceased during the night, and the sun rose clear, and shone uninterruptedly during the day. The morning was cold, but the snow commenced thawing about nine o'clock, and continued till a little after three, when it commenced freezing. The river, which was open on our arrival, is now covered with ice, except where there are ripples. Employed in exploring the adjacent country and the mines. In the afternoon, selecting specimens of ore, and building a small furnace for smelting lead, as the hunters are desirous of supplying themselves with bullets. Killed two deer and one wolf.

MONDAY, JAN. 4TH.

It began snowing a little after midnight, and continued until day-break. Engaged in digging at the mines, and viewing the country. The prairies, which commence at the distance of a mile west of this river, are the most extensive, rich, and beautiful, of any which I have ever seen west of the Mississippi river. They are covered by a coarse wild grass, which attains so great a height that it completely hides a man on horseback in riding through it. The deer and elk abound in this quarter, and the buffaloe is occasionally seen in droves upon the prairies, and in the open high-land woods. Along the margin of the river, and to a width of from one to two miles each way, is found a vigorous growth of forest-trees, some of which attain an almost incredible size. The lands consist of a rich black alluvial soil, apparently deep, and calculated for corn, flax, and hemp. The river-banks are skirted with cane, to the exclusion of all other underbrush; and the lands rise gently from the river for a mile, terminating in high-lands, without bluffs, with a handsome growth of hickory and oak, and a soil which is probably adapted for wheat, rye, oats, and potatoes. Little prairies of a mile or two in extent are sometimes seen in the midst of a heavy forest, resembling some old cultivated field, which has been suffered to run into grass.

Near our present encampment are some bluffs, which serve to diversify the scene, and at the foot of which is situated a valuable lead-mine. A country thus situated, cannot fail to present a scene of great beauty in the season of verdure, and even now, in the depth of winter, wears a pleasing aspect. It is a mixture of forest and plain, of hills and long sloping valleys, where the tall oak forms a striking contrast with the rich foliage of the evergreen cane, or the waving field prairie-grass. It is an assemblage of beautiful groves, and level prairies, of river alluvion, and high-land precipice, diversified by the devious course of the river, and the distant promontory, forming a scene so novel, yet so harmonious, as to strike the beholder with admiration; and the effect must be greatly heightened, when viewed under the influence of a mild clear atmosphere, and an invigorating sun, such as is said to characterize this region during the spring and summer. Taking these circumstances into veiw, with the fertility and extent of soil, its advantages for water-carriage, and other objects, among which its mines deserve to be noticed, it offers great attractions to enterprizing emigrants, and particularly to such as may consider great prospective advantages an equivalent for the dangers and privations of a frontier settlement. The junction of Findley's Fork with James' River, a high, rich point of land, is an eligible spot for a town, and the erection of a new county out of this part of the unincorporated wilderness of Arkansaw, would soon give the settlers the advantages elsewhere enjoyed in civil communities. A profitable fur-trade would be one of the immediate advantages attending such a settlement. Both the Osage and Cherokee nations would soon be drawn to this spot, as the most eligible and convenient point for trading; also, a part of the Pawnees, and some scattered bands of the Delawares and Shawanees of Missouri Territory. A water-communication exists with the Mississippi. Steamboats may ascend White River to the mouth of its Great North Fork. Keel-boats of twenty tons burthen may, during the greater part of the year, ascend to the mouth of James' River; and boats of eight tons burthen may ascend that to the junction of Findley's Fork, about fifteen miles below our present spot of encampment, to which the navigation may be continued in smaller boats, thus establishing a communication by which the peltries, the lead, and the agricultural products of the country, could be easily, cheaply, and at all seasons, taken to market, and merchandize brought up in return.

Having now satisfied ourselves with respect to the objects of our tour, and the weather rendering a further residence unpleasant, it is determined to begin our journey back to-morrow.

TUESDAY, JAN. 5TH.

At an early hour, and before the dawn of day, we arose, and began to prepare the last meal we were to partake of on the banks of James' River, and to put ourselves in readiness to leave a camp, and a country which had already became so familiar to us as to appear, in some measure, a home. After breakfast, the hunters went down the river about a mile to bring up their horses, who had, on our arrival, been turned to feed in a cane-brake at that distance. While they were absent, we arranged our travelling packs both for the horses and ourselves, a service in which we had at this time become adepts; and having leisure, while we awaited their return, which was protracted a considerable time by not finding the horses where expected, we blazed a large tree of the species *quercus tinctoria,* that stood near to our camp, and engraved thereon our names, with the date of our visit. Other evidences of our visit to, and occupation of the country, were left in the camp we had erected, the trees we had cut, the furnace put up for smelting ore; and the pits sunk in search of it, &c. At seven o'clock we were ready to commence our return, and crossing the river, a little above our encampment, pursued a south course for the Hunters' Cabins on White River. There was still snow upon the ground, a part of which had fallen during the preceding night, and its whole depth was from two to three inches, lying pretty compact, and somewhat moist, so that the tracks of deer and other animals were plainly imprinted upon it, and if our design had been hunting, these traces would have surely directed us in the pursuit. We were surprised, in fact, by the innumerable tracks of the deer, wolf, elk, bear, and turkey, met with, the snow being completely trodden down in many places with them, and affording a perfect map of their movements. In several instances we observed the places where deer had lain down the night of the snow, the shape of the animal in a reclining posture being left upon the dry leaves, while the surrounding country was covered with snow to a depth of two or three inches. It was evident the animal had lain still during the fall of snow, and arose after it had ceased. These places of rest were located in the open woods, and on the declivities of hills. Though several were passed, I observed none in any other situation, and no protection against the wind or weather was afforded by underbrush, the country being of that open nature which is in a great degree destitute of bushes or shrubbery. It is probable, however, that this animal in seeking rest at night, chooses that part of a hill which is situated opposite to the point from which the wind, at the time of its lying down, blows, and which is sheltered by the intervening eminence. I am not in possession of a sufficient number of facts to determine this point, which would give to the deer a degree of sagacity that it had not, heretofore, been supposed to possess; but such facts as I do possess go to establish this position. The resting-spots, here noticed, were uniformly situated on south-west declivities. The snow-storm came from the north-east.

Frequently we crossed wolf-trails in the snow, and in one or two instances observed spots where they had apparently played, or fought with each other, like a large pack of dogs, the snow being trod down in a circle of great extent. The turkey, so numerous in this region, had also been driven out of the adjoining valleys of James and Findley Rivers, by the recent snow, in search of food, and we passed over tracts where, for many acres together, the snow was scratched up by this bird to procure the acorns, and the green leaves, roots, and grass below. Our progress being attended with some noise, the game fled at our approach, and either kept out of our sight, or out of the reach of our guns. The deer, however, which is very abundant, was frequently in view, and we sometimes started droves of twenty or thirty at a time. Being suddenly aroused, no animal surpasses the deer in fleetness, and I have enjoyed a high gratification in surveying a frightened troop of them in full speed across an extensive prairie, or barren open woods, where they could be observed for a mile, or more. They will bound twenty feet at a leap, on a gentle declivity. This I have afterwards measured.

The deer, however, has a fatal curiosity, which prompts it, after running five or six hundred yards, to turn around and look back upon its pursuer, and it is at this moment that he is killed. For the hunter, on starting a deer, immediately pursues with all his speed after it, without regarding the noise made among the bushes and upon the earth; for a similar disturbance, excited by the deer itself, prevents it from distinguishing that of its pursuer, and whenever it stops to turn around, at that instant also the hunter is still, and if within shooting distance, say one hundred yards, he fires; but if not, he endeavors to creep up, by skulking behind bushes and trees. If, in this attempt, he is discovered, and the deer takes the alarm, he again follows in the pursuit, assured that it will, in running a certain distance, again turn round and stand still to see whether it is pursued. This extraordinary and fatal curiosity is the cause of so many of these animals being killed, for did they rely unhesitatingly upon that strength and activity of limb with which nature has so admirably provided them for running, no foot-hunter, and no dog, would be able to overtake them.

About noon we reached and forded Findley's Fork, a stream we had encamped upon, in our journey west, on the last day of December. Two miles beyond, in ascending a valley, we discovered a bee-tree, which Mr. Pettibone and myself chopped down. It was a large white oak, *(quercus alba,)* two and-an-half feet across at the butt, and contained, in a hollow limb, several gallons of honey. This was the first discovery of wild honey which accident had thrown in our way, and as soon as the saccharine treasure was laid bare, by cutting open the hollow limb, we began unceremoniously to partake. And although two months' residence in the woods had left little in our personal appearance, or mode of living, to denote our acquaintance with polished society; and our appetites, by continual exercise, the want of vegetable food, and sometimes the total want of food of any kind for one, two, and even three days together, had become voracious and gross, to a degree that excited our own astonishment; yet, when we retired a few yards to view the beastly voraciousness and savage deportment of the two hunters during this sweet quaternary repast, we could not resist the most favourable conclusions concerning our own deportment, and physical decorum upon that occasion. It should here be remarked, that the white hunters in this region, (and I am informed it is the same with the Indians,) are passionately fond of wild honey, and whenever a tree containing it is found, it is the custom to assemble around it, and feast, even to a surfeit. Upon the present occasion we had no bread, which, although it prevented us from partaking so liberally as we otherwise should, did not seem in any degree to operate as a restraint upon them. On the contrary, they ate prodigiously. Each stood with a long comb of honey, elevated with both hands, in front of the mouth, and at every bite left the semi-circular dented impression of a capacious jaw, while the exterior muscles of the throat and face were swelled by their incessant exertions to force down the unmasticated lumps of honey, which rapidly followed each other into the natural repository—the stomach. When this scene of gluttony was ended, the dog also received his share, as the joint co-partner and sharer of the fatigues, dangers, and enjoyments of the chace; and in no instance have we observed this compact between the dog and the hunter to have been violated, for it is recorded in a manner less subject to obliteration or distinction than our

Aerial view of Logan's Ridge, Bull Creek vicinity, Christian County, Missouri, circa 1985. Cleared ridges and forested slopes are typical of many hill districts in the Ozarks. PHOTOGRAPH BY MILTON RAFFERTY.

fugitive agreements upon paper; it is recorded among the powerful habits of uncivilized man, corporeally and mentally imprinted. The honey then left was tied up in a wet deer-skin, which communicates no taint; and, appended to the saddle of one of the horses, thus carried along. We now emerged from the valley into a level plain moderately elevated, covered with white and black oak, and some underbrush, with a soil susceptible of cultivation, destitute, however, of streams; and sufficiently open to admit of easy travelling. Toward evening we descried, on our right, a valley heavily wooded, and bending off toward the south; and, presuming it to be the valley of Swan Creek, descended into, and pursued it down for two or three miles, and encamped. Distance twenty miles. Killed one deer. Weather moderately cold. The sun has not been sufficiently powerful to melt the snow so as to produce water, but has softened the surface of it a little in exposed situations.

WEDNESDAY, JAN. 6TH.

We were deceived in the valley which we yesterday entered. Instead of Swan, it proved to be Bull Creek, also a tributary to White River; but which we should have headed, leaving it wholly on our right, as it is universally known among hunters, and avoided, as a hilly, sterile region, and which, from the similarity in the natural phisiognomy of the hills, trees, soil, and brush, is considered a dangerous place to get lost in, particularly in foggy weather, when the sun cannot be seen. Of the justice of this impression, our journey this day has afforded conclusive proof, being foiled in several successive attempts to cross the adjoining high-lands, and returned upon it, at different places, by its lateral valleys. Thus we spent one half of the day in vain and perplexing endeavours, wandering from one high knoll to another; and, at length, by a lucky hit, succeeded in reaching one of the tributary streams of Swan Creek, upon which, after following it down for several miles, we encamped; distance ten miles. In passing down Bull Creek, and in some places along the valley in which we are now encamped, the tracks of bear upon the snow, some of enormous size, have been very plentifully observed; but as hunting is not our object, we have not pursued them to the dens, and to the hollow trees, into which they have, at this season, retired. These traces, made upon the snow, in the most inclement part of a Missouri winter, show conclusively, that although this animal retires, on the approach of snow and cold weather, into crevices, caves, and fissures in the rock, and into large hollow trees, and other places where he can lie secure and warm; and can there subsist a length of time upon the superabundant fat with which nature has provided him for that purpose, and without any other nutriment; yet he occasionally quits those recesses, and seeks food upon the adjoining plains. It is probable, also, that he frequently changes the place of retirement during the winter-season, and only ventures out of his hiding-place in the mildest days, and at noon, when the power of the sun is at its maximum of heat upon the earth. Hunters kill this animal during the winter-season by tracking him up to his den, either upon the snow, or by the scent of dogs. If tracked to a large cave, they enter, and often find him in its farthest recess, when he is shot without farther difficulty. If a narrow aperture in the rock, dogs are sent in to provoke him to battle; thus he is either brought in sight within the cave, or driven entirely out of it, and while engaged with the dogs, the hunter walks up deliberately to within a few feet, and pierces him through the heart. A shot through the flank, thigh, shoulder, or even the neck, does not kill him, but provokes him to the utmost rage, and sometimes four or five shots are necessary to kill him; for, as he is constantly in motion, it is very improbable that the first shot, however sure the rifle from which it is driven, will penetrate the heart; and it is not uncommon that one, two, or three of the best dogs are killed in the affray, either by the bear, or a mistaken shot from the huntsman, in which case the bear taken by no means compensates for the dogs lost; for a high value is set upon a good dog, and his death is greatly lamented. Neither is such a dog soon forgotten; and his achievements in the chace, his deep-mouthed cry, his agility and fleetness, his daring attack, and desperate gnash, and his dexterity in avoiding the fatal paw of his antagonist, these long continue to be the theme of admiration. When seated around his cabin-fire, the old hunter excites the wonder of his credulous children, gathered into a groupe, to listen to the recital of his youthful deeds, and thus creates in their breasts a desire to follow the same pursuits, and to excel in those hunting exploits which command the universal applause of their companions, and crown with fancied glory the life of the transalleganian hunter, whether red or white.

In the course of the last two days we have also passed, upon different streams, the habitations of the beaver, an animal so highly valued for its fur, and which differs from other quadrupeds in having chosen that part of the vegetable creation for its sustenance which is rejected by all others, viz. the bark of trees. To procure this, it is provided with two large teeth in the under-jaw, set with astonishing firmness, and resembling chissels, by which it is enabled to gnaw or cut down saplings, and even large trees. These, when down, they completely peel, preferring, however, the bark of the smaller limbs and twigs, which are young, tender, and full of sap. Often they so contrive it as to make them fall into the water, where they serve to stop and collect all floating limbs and brush, making a kind of dam, which thus supplies them with food without the labour, (and an immense labour it must be) of gnawing down large trees. There are few descriptions of wood, the bark of which they will not eat. Thus they attack the maple, the mulberry, black walnut, and elm; nor does the astringent and bitter properties of the oak prevent them from making it an article of food. They prefer, however, all barks which have an aromatic, or spicy flavour, and from the number of those trees we find peeled, possess a high relish for several kinds of laurus, which abound in the valleys in this region, particularly spice-wood and sassafras. Being web-footed, their favourite region is the water, and they seldom venture far from the banks of the stream they inhabit, and never travel on to the neighbouring high-lands. They burrow in the banks of the stream above the water level, so that they lie dry: but the mouths of their habitations are situated below the waters, so that it enters them for a distance, and they cannot get out without diving into the water. By this sagacious contrivance they at once exclude the cold air from their habitations, and prevent their being entered by animals which cannot endure to live under water. It is probable many of their natural enemies are thus debarred of their prey. As all other species of animated nature, which has been endowed with sufficient sagacity and foresight for its own preservation by habits and customs peculiar to itself, is also endowed with some peculiar tastes, habits, or propensities, which are prone to work its own destruction; so the beaver, which has wisdom enough to cut down trees and form dams, and elude the vigilance of its enemies, both man and beast, in an hundred ways, yet falls a sacrifice to its passion for high sweet-scented herbs, and spicy barks. It is by a skilful preparation of these, that beaver-trappers are enabled to take such quantities of them. A natural musky substance, taken from the stomach of the beaver, serves as the principal article in the composition of the bait which is put into the trap; some sassafras, and other barks and fragrant herbs, are added; the exact proportions and method of preparation being a secret only known to those who are skilled in trapping, and who are unwilling to communicate the information.

THURSDAY, JAN. 7TH.

The atmosphere, on encamping last night, was clouded up for a change of weather, which we were fearful would prove rain, but a little after midnight it commenced snowing, and continued without intermission until day-light, and at different periods, until four o'clock in the afternoon. Lying down considerably fatigued, we slept soundly, and did not discover the snow until it had fallen some depth upon us, and although I could not relish sleep under such circumstances, both my companion and the hunters maintained their positions upon the ground until near day-light, when the snow had attained a depth of several inches. We now followed down the valley in which we had encamped about eight miles, in which distance it opened into the valley of Swan Creek, and we found ourselves about ten miles above its junction with White River, upon the banks of this large and beautiful stream, which is richly entitled to the appellation of a river. Some doubt arose here as to the proper course of travelling, the day being cloudy, and the atmos-

Aerial view of cleared land in the White River hills region, circa 1990. Thousands of acres of scrubby woodland have been cleared and planted to grass for pasture.
PHOTOGRAPH BY MILTON RAFFERTY.

phere obscured with snow; but, in travelling a few miles south, we were rejoiced to find ourselves in sight of the Bald-hill, a well-known land-mark to the hunter in this region, and which I have already alluded to in my journey west. Toward this we steered undeviatingly, without regard to the steepness of the intervening hills or valleys, or the scraggy brush that opposed our progress, and falling into our old trail at its foot, pursued with an accelerated pace toward the Hunters' Cabins. Snow had, however, so much obliterated the track, that we were unable long to continue in it; and, as the thick and clouded state of the atmosphere prevented our guides from judging of our position, we soon became completely lost. In this dilemma, recourse was had to a very novel experiment, and in which I confess I had but little faith. One of the hunters happened to be riding a horse, which he said had, two or three times, on similar occasions, on being left to take his own course, brought him safely either in some well-known spot in the woods where he had before encamped, or to his own house. He determined again to make

Aerial view of Dewey Bald near Branson, Missouri, circa 1970. This bald knob, one of many in the White River hills, was made famous in Harold Bell Wright's novel, Shepherd of the Hills. PHOTOGRAPH BY MILTON RAFFERTY.

trial of the horse's sagacity, and throwing the reins loose upon its neck, the animal took its own course, sometimes climbing up hills, then descending into valleys, or crossing over streams, and at last, to the infinite satisfaction of all, and to the surprise of myself and co-travellers, led us to the top of a commanding precipice which overlooked the valley of White River, with its heavy-wooded forest, the towering bluffs on its south-western verge, with the river winding along at their base, and the hunters' cottages, indicated by the curling smoke among the trees, in plain perspective. Joy sparkled in every eye; we stood a moment to contemplate the sublime and beautiful scene before us, which was such an assemblage of rocks and water—of hill and valley—of verdant woods and naked peaks—of native fertility and barren magnificence, as to surpass the boldest conceptions, and most happy executions of the painter's pencil, or the poet's pen. The reins were now resumed, and as we descended the bluff the hunter lavished great encomiums on the sagacity and faithfulness of his horse, whose pedigree and biography we were now entertained with. In due course of narration, it was shown where the horse had originated, what masters he had been subject to, how he could live in the woods without feed, how long he had been the fortunate owner of him, what "hair-breadth escapes" he had made upon his back, &c. &c. All this was mixed with abundance of the most tedious, trifling, and fatiguing particulars, communicated in bad grammar, wretchedly pronounced, so that we were heartily glad when he had arrived at the conclusion, that he was an animal of uncommon sagacity, strength, activity, and worth. For, as in most other biographies, all these words had been wasted to prove the existence of wisdom where it never was, and to make us admire worth which nobody had ever discovered. The end of this dissertation, that had only been interrupted by the occasional stumbling of the beast itself, (which was in reality a most sorry jade,) brought us to within half-a-mile of their cabins, when they both discharged their rifles to advertise their families of our near approach, and in a few moments we were welcomed by dogs, women, and children, all greasy and glad, to the nailless habitations of our conductors. Distance twenty miles.

FRIDAY, JAN. 8TH.

Once more arrived at the spot where circumstances had condemned us to perform a kind of quarantine during sixteen days on our journey westward, every object appeared familiar to us, and the very stumps and trees around the house, and the lofty spiral rocks which towered in front, seemed objects with which we had enjoyed immemorial familiarity, and contributed in some degree to that buoyancy of spirit which is so natural on the accomplishment of an undertaking, which has been approached with fatigue, and attained with difficulty; for they were regarded as the silent witnesses of some of the most painful of those difficulties and fatigues, and served to awaken a train of reflections and comparisons which were at once exhilarating and satisfactory. We had already determined on returning to Potosi by a different route from that pursued on our outward journey, as well to diversify the tour, as to avoid the distressing situations to which we were often reduced in passing through the wilderness. It only remained to decide upon the route which promised to afford the most interesting field for observation; and both on that account, as well as uniting greater conveniences in travelling, the descent by White River by water seemed to possess decided advantages. We lost no time, therefore, in preparing for our descent, feeling an anxiety to return, which was much heightened by the reflection that we had already consumed more time than we had allotted ourselves for the performance of the entire journey on quitting Potosi, and that our friends would be ready to conclude we had fallen a sacrifice to the dangers of a tour, which few had approbated as adviseable in the outset, and all united in considering as very hazardous.

V

Down the White River from the Beaver Creek Settlement to Poke Bayou

SATURDAY, JAN. 9TH.

Having, in pursuance of this determination, purchased a canoe of the hunters, and made other necessary preparations, we were ready at an early hour in the morning to embark. We now found it necessary again to resume the use of our guns, after having for nearly a month been supplied with provisions by the hunters, and for that purpose had procured a quantity of lead and ball. We also put into our canoe some bear's meat smoked, dried venison, corn-bread, and salt, with a few articles reserved from our former pack, which were either necessary or convenient on encamping. The men, women, and children, followed us down to the shore, and after giving us many directions and precautions, and repeating their wishes for our success, we bid them adieu, and shoving our canoe into the stream, found ourselves, with a little exertion of paddles, flowing at the rate of from three to four miles per hour down one of the most beautiful and enchanting rivers which discharge their waters into the Mississippi. To a width and a depth which entitles it to be classed as a river of the third magnitude in western America, it unites a current which possesses the purity of crystal, with a smooth and gentle flow, and the most imposing, diversified, and delightful scenery. Its shores are composed of smooth spherical and angular pieces of opaque, red, and white gravel, consisting of water-worn fragments of carbonate of lime, hornstone, quartz, and jasper. Every pebble, rock, fish, or floating body, either animate or inanimate, which occupies the bottom of the stream, is seen while passing over it with the most perfect accuracy; and our canoe often seemed as if suspended in air, such is the remarkable transparency of the water. Sometimes the river for many miles washed the base of a wall of calcareous rock, rising to an enormous height, and terminating in spiral, broken, and miniform masses, in the fissures of which the oak and the cedar had forced their crooked roots, and hung in a threatening posture above us. Perched upon these, the eagle, hawk, turkey, and heron, surveyed our approach without alarm, secure in eminent distance. Facing such rocks, the corresponding curve of the river invariably presented a level plain of rich alluvial soil, covered with a vigorous growth of forest-trees, cane, shrubs, and vines, and affording a most striking contrast to the sterile grandeur on the opposite shore. Here the paths of the deer and buffaloe, where they daily came down to drink, were numerous all along the shore, and the former we frequently surprised as he stood in silent security upon the river's brink. The duck, brant, and goose, continually rose in flocks before us, and alighting in the stream a short distance below, were soon again aroused by our approach; thus we often drove them down the river for many hours together, until our repeated intrusion at last put them to effectual flight. Often a lofty ridge of rocks in perspective seemed to oppose a barrier to the further progress of the river, which suddenly turned away in the most unexpected direction at the moment we reached the fancied barrier, displaying to our view other groupes of rocks, forests, plains, and shores, arranged in the most singular and fantastic manner, and in the utmost apparent confusion, but which, on a nearer inspection, developed a beautiful order and corresponding regularity, such as the intelligent mind constantly observes in the physiognomy of nature, and which appears the more surprising the more minutely it is inspected, analyzed, or compared. Very serpentine in its course, the river carried us toward every point of the compass in the course of the day; sometimes rocks skirted one shore, sometimes the other, never both at the same place, but rock and alluvion generally alternating from one side to the other, the bluffs being much variegated in their exterior form, extent, and relative position, giving perpetual novelty to the scenery, which ever excited fresh interest and renewed gratification, so that we saw the sun sink gradually in the west without being tired of viewing the mingled beauty, grandeur, barrenness, and fertility, as displayed by the earth, rocks, air, water, light, trees, sky, and animated nature; they form the ever-winding, diversified, and enchanting banks of White River.

A short distance below the Hunters' Cabins we passed the mouth of Beaver Creek, a clear stream of thirty yards wide, entering from the left, and

remarkable for the number of beavers formerly caught in it. As night overtook us, we descried on the left bank of the river a hunter's cabin, which we
found in the occupation of a person of the name of Yochem, who readily
gave us permission to remain for the night, having descended the river thirty
miles. Here, among other wild meats, we were invited at supper, as a particular mark of respect, to partake of a roasted beaver's tail, one of the greatest dainties known to the Missouri hunter. Having heard much said among
hunters concerning the peculiar flavour and delicious richness of this dish,
I was highly gratified in having an opportunity of judging for myself, and
accepted with avidity the offer of our host. The tail of this animal, unlike
every other part of it, and of every other animal of the numerous tribe of
quadrupeds, is covered with a thick scaly skin, resembling in texture certain fish, and in shape analogous to a paper-folder, or the bow of a lady's
corset, tapering a little toward the end, and pyramidal on the lateral edges.
It is cooked by roasting before the fire, when the skin peals off, and it is eaten
simply with salt. It has a mellow, luscious taste, melting in the mouth somewhat like marrow, and being in taste something intermediate between that
and a boiled perch. To this compound flavour of fish and marrow it has, in
the way in which hunters eat it, a slight disagreeable smell of oil. Could this
be removed by some culinary process, it would undoubtedly be received on
the table of the epicure with great eclat.

SUNDAY, JAN. 10TH.

Leaving the hunter's cabin at an early hour, we passed, at the distance of
two miles below, the mouth of Bear Creek, a long, narrow, crooked stream,
coming in on the right. Near its head, the hunters procure flints for their
rifles. Toward evening we passed a hunter's cabin on our right, and about
two miles below another on our left, where we concluded to stop for the
night, and found it to be the habitation of a Mr. Coker, by whom we were
entertained thirty-one days ago on our journey up. He appeared pleased at
our return, and our success. Distance twenty-five miles.

MONDAY, JAN. 11TH.

It rained hard during the night, but ceased a little before day-break, when
we embarked in our canoe, and descended the river forty miles. This
brought us to M'Gary's, where we first struck White River, on crossing the

wilderness from Potosi, and where, on the 8th December, we left our horse, and a part of our travelling pack. Sixteen miles below Coker's, alias Sugar-Loaf Prairie, we passed the mouth of Big Creek, a stream of thirty yards wide, entering on the left. Two or three hunters had just located themselves at this place, and were engaged in cutting down trees, and building a house, as we passed. Immediately after passing Big Creek, we met a petty trader coming up stream with a large canoe, in which he had the remains of a barrel of whiskey, and a few other articles intended to be bartered off for skins among the hunters. Of him, anxious to hear how the civilized world was progressing, we inquired the news, but were disappointed to learn that he himself resided at no great distance below, where he had purchased his articles from another trader, and knew nothing of those political occurrences in our own country, about which we felt solicitous to be informed. He evinced, indeed, a perfect indifference to those things, and hardly comprehended the import of such inquiries. He knew, forsooth, that he was living under the United States' government, and had some indefinite ideas about St. Louis, New Orleans, and Washington; but who filled the presidential chair, what Congress were deliberating upon, whether the people of Missouri had been admitted to form a state, constitution, and government, and other analogous matters, these were subjects which, to use his own phraseology, "he had never troubled his head about." Such a total ignorance of the affairs of his own country, and indifference to passing events, in one who possessed enterprise enough to become a river pedlar, surprised us, even here, in this benighted corner of the union. After a confabulation of fifteen or twenty minutes, we parted, he urging his heavy canoe with labour up stream, and we descending with an easy motion of the paddle in the current, which had now imperceptibly acquired greater velocity, and we found ourselves passing with rapidity over the Pot Shoals, a gentle rapid in the river, of which we had been advised, and where, from the descriptions given, we were prepared to encounter difficulties which we did not meet. In passing seven miles below these shoals, we came in view of a high wall of rocks on the left shore, which we recognized as being situated immediately opposite M'Gary's, where we arrived as day-light threw its last faint corruscations from the west. At the foot of this bluff, and directly in front of M'Gary's, the Little North Fork of White River discharges itself into the main stream, being at the point of junction about fifty yards wide. It is a river estimated to be 100 miles in length, may be ascended a considerable distance with light water-craft, and has some rich alluvion near its mouth, but originates in, and runs chiefly through, a barren region. This is the stream upon whose banks we encamped on the 6th of December, while sojourning in the wilderness, between the great north and south branches of White River.

TUESDAY, JAN. 12TH.

We were cordially welcomed at M'Gary's, and congratulated on our perseverance in visiting a region where travelling was, in their estimation, attended with so much hazard from Indian hostility, and our progress to which had been attended with such accumulated difficulties. They had heard of our two weeks' probation at Holt and Fisher's cabins, during which we had been employed upon their habitations, and in chopping wood, &c. and considered it as an unmanly advantage taken of our situation. On learning from us that the Osage Indians had broken up their hunting encampments in the region about James' River, and retired upon the Grand Osage some weeks previous to our arrival, one of the sons of M'Gary manifested a strong inclination to go out upon a hunting excursion into that quarter, which, on further learning that we had found game abundant, he immediately determined upon, and was ready to set out toward that country at the time we embarked in our canoe this morning. Undoubtedly he will be rewarded with as many skins as he can transport back. In our descent this day, we have passed several hunters' cabins on both banks of the river, but met nothing worthy particular note until our arrival at the Bull Shoals, situated twenty miles below M'Gary's. Here the river has a fall of fifteen or twenty feet in the distance of half-a-mile, and stands full of rugged calcareous rocks, among which the water foams and rushes with astonishing velocity and incessant noise. There are a hundred channels, and the strange navigator runs an imminent risk of being dashed upon the rocks, or sunk beneath the waves, whose whirling boiling and unceasing roar warns him of his peril long before he reaches the rapids. There is a channel through which canoes and even large boats pass with a good depth of water, but being unacquainted with it, we ran the hazard of being sunk, and found our canoe drawn rapidly into the suction of the falls, apprehensive of the result. In a few moments, notwithstanding every effort to keep our barque headed downwards, the conflicting eddies drove us against a rock, and we were instantly thrown broadside upon the rugged peaks which stand thickly in the swiftest part of the first schute, or fall. Luckily it did not fill, but the pressure of the current against a canoe thirty feet in length, lying across the stream, was more than we could counteract, and we had nearly exhausted our strength in vain endeavours to extricate and aright it. For all this time we were in the water, at a depth of two, three, and four feet, at a cool January temperature, but at length succeeded in lifting it over a ledge of rocks, and again got afloat. We now shot down the current rapidly and undisturbed for 600 yards, which brought us to the verge of the second schute, where we twice encountered a similar difficulty, but succeeded, with analogous efforts, in passing our canoe and effects in safety. This is the most considerable obstruction to the navigation of the river we have yet encountered, but is said to be perfectly safe in high tides, when the rocks are buried by the vernal and autumnal floods. At these shoals lead ore (galena,) is found in small lumps, adhering to the rocks in the river and on the shores, with some calcareous spar; and the banks are further rendered interesting by some remains of ancient works, which appear to indicate that it has been the seat of metallurgical operations in former ages, and previous to the deposition of the alluvial soil upon its banks, for beneath this soil are imbedded the *reliqua* in question. Thus imbedded masses of a metallic alloy, manifestly the production of art, with bits of earthen pots, and arrow-heads chipped out of flint, horn-stone, and jasper, are found. The metallic alloy appears, from hardness and colour, to be lead united with silver or tin. It is not well refined, although it may be easily cut with a knife. The earthenware appears to have been submitted to the action of fire, and has suffered no decay. Of all these I procured specimens, of which duplicates are to be seen among the collections of Dr. Samuel L. Mitchill, at New-York.

Having spent some time in our passage over the rapids, and got thoroughly wetted, so that we felt chilly and uncomfortable, we determined to stop at the next cabin which presented itself on the banks of the river. This happened to be the house of Augustine Friend, situated five miles below the shoals, a man of some intelligence, and who has the honour of giving name to a settlement which is forming around him. By him we were treated with much hospitality, and furnished with several facts relative to the geography and productions of the surrounding country. Being an enterprising hunter, as well as a farmer, he has visited the most remote parts of the White River country, and has traversed the region we have just explored. He represents the existence of rock-salt, between the head of the south fork of White River and the Arkansaw; that the Pawnees and Osage Indians make use of it, and that he has seen, and used it, and says it is clear like alum. He is acquainted with the lead-mines on James' River, and represents the bod-

Bull Shoals Dam and Lake. COURTESY OF THE ARKANSAS DEPARTMENT OF PARKS AND TOURISM.

ies of ore as very great; and says that the Pawnee mountains, situated south of the Grand Osage River, afford beautiful black and white marble. Mr. Friend has lately been detained a prisoner by the Osages; but although they stole his beaver traps, and some other articles, he was treated humanely in other respects, and suffered, after a confinement of several weeks, to depart. In relating the particulars of his captivity, and in repeating several anecdotes illustrative of savage life and manners, the time passed imperceptibly away, so that although wet and fatigued on our arrival, it was after ten before we betook ourselves to rest.

WEDNESDAY, JAN. 13TH.

Mr. Friend having represented the antiquities in that neighbourhood as worthy of examination, together with the mineral appearances on the hills, situated back from the river, we determined to devote a part of the day to that object. The hills, like every other section of this country noticed, proved stratified masses of secondary lime-stone, covered by a deposit of elder alluvion, the surface of which afforded radiated quartz, and fragments of hornstone, but no particular indications of a metalliferous character were observed. The antiquities, situated principally on the east bank of the river, at the Bull Shoals, have already been mentioned. Some further appearances of this kind are seen at the distance of a half-a-mile below the dwelling of Mr. Friend, where I procured an excellent kind of flint, and some antique bones and arrow-heads, from beneath a heavy bed of alluvion covered by trees. Owing to these little excursions, it was late before we left Friend's settlement. Four miles below we stopped at a Mr. Lee's, being the first Yankee met with in these regions; and, after dinner, went down the river about six miles to J. Yochem's, where we passed the night.

THURSDAY, JAN. 14TH.

Here we concluded to lend our canoe to Mr. Yochem, who in addition to his own, stood in need of it, to carry down bears bacon and pork, to a trader lying at the mouth of the Great North Fork, of whom he had made some purchases. The distance was computed at thirty-five miles by water, and included some of the most difficult navigation in the river, while by land it was only fifteen. Leaving our baggage therefore to be brought down in the canoe, we took a foot or horse-path leading across the country, and arrived a little before night on the banks of the river, opposite Matney's, at the mouth of the Great North Fork. But we were separated from his house by the river, which was wide and deep; and having no canoe to cross, there seemed no hesitation between lying in the woods, and wading through the river, which we found about four feet deep in the shallowest place, and reached Matney's just at dusk, wet and chilly. Our canoe did not arrive that night. This we attributed to the difficulty in passing two formidable shoals above. The first is situated fifteen miles below J. Yochem's, and is called the Crooked Creek Shoals, being immediately at the mouth of Crooked Creek, a long and devious stream, coming in on the right or south side of the river. The second shoal is five miles lower, and is called the Buffalo Shoals, being situated at the mouth of the Buffalo Fork of White River. This is a large stream, also entering on the south side of the river. It originates near the north banks of the Arkansaw, and is about 180 miles in length. Its banks afford some rich alluvion, and it is a region much resorted to by hunters on account of the abundance of game it affords. The shoals at its mouth are considered the most formidable obstacle to the navigation of White River, and although boats pass and repass at certain stages of water, it may be reckoned an effectual interruption to navigation for all boats over eight tons. From the foot of these shoals, however, to its junction with the Mississippi, the navigation of White River is unobstructed, and the largest keel-boats, barges, and even steam-boats, may in safety ascend, particularly up to the Great North Fork, which enters on the north, about half-a-mile below the spot where we now tarry. There is now a keel boat lying here, which ascended a few weeks ago on a trading voyage among the hunters and farmers. It is a boat of thirty tons burthen, built at Pittsburgh, and decked and painted off in the neat and convenient style of the generality of Ohio and Mississippi boats of her class, but is prevented from going higher by the Buffalo Shoals. The articles brought up in it, for the purposes of exchange, were chiefly flour, salt, and whiskey, with some coffee, calico, and a few smaller articles. In return, beaver, deer, otter, bear, and raccoon skins, bears' bacon, fresh pork, and beef, in the gross, venison, bees'-wax, honey, and buffalo beef, are taken. From the rates of exchange noticed, I concluded a trading-voyage on this stream is attended with immense profit.

Friday, Jan. 15th.

Compelled, by the non-arrival of our canoe, to spend the day at this spot, I determined to improve the time by a ramble through the adjacent country, and to seek that amusement in the examination of rocks, and trees, and mountain-scenery, which was neither to be found in conversation with the inmates of the house, nor in any other way. The natural appearances of surrounding objects wore an interesting character, and though detained here by accident, a diligent search of the whole river could not in all probability have afforded a point uniting, in the circle of a few miles, so many objects calculated to please the eye, or to instruct the understanding. To a geographical situation, the most important in the whole course of the river, it united scenery the most bold and enchanting, and embracing so many objects calculated to awaken and invite attention, that the inquiring traveller could scarcely be disappointed, be his studies or pursuits what they might. Here were beautiful views for the landscape-painter, rocks for the geologist, minerals and fossils for the mineralogist, trees and plants for the botanist, soil for the agriculturist, an advantageous situation for the man of business, and a gratifying view for the patriot, who contemplates with pleasure the increasing settlement, and prospective improvements of our country. Here, the innumerable streams which originate in a district of country 400 miles long, by 200 in breadth, collected into two large and beautiful rivers, unite, and from this point forth to the Mississippi, form a river navigable at all seasons, for boats of the largest burden. From the north, from the south, and from the west of this tract, from the most noted, and from its most unfrequented corners, we here behold the assembled tributaries, flowing in a smooth, broad, deep, and majestic current, between banks of the richest alluvion, covered with the most vigorous growth of vegetable life, and skirted at a short distance by mountains of the most imposing grandeur. But although composed of streams, which originate in sections of country, differing widely in point of fertility, and other natural properties, yet there is a remarkable agreement in that character, most obvious to the sight, its extreme limpidity and want of colour, and which was early seized upon by the French traders on first visiting this stream, in calling it La Rivière Blanche, (White River,) in allusion to the purity of its water.

With such an assemblage of interesting objects around me, I sauntered out to take a nearer view of the face of nature, and spent the day along the shores of the river, in the contiguous forest, or on the naked peaks of the neighbouring hills. The water of the river, at this season of the year, has retired below its banks to its lowest mark, which is about fifteen feet below its flood height, and exposes a high alluvial shore, and a wide gravelly beach on both sides. Here a margin of clean gravel, washed by the water into fanciful piles, and of every shape and colour, affords a delightful and uninterrupted walk for many miles, and by its ever-winding course, and diversified scenery, keeps the eye in continual expectation of something new or interesting, and lightens the fatigue experienced at every step by sinking shoe-deep into the gravel. I amused myself by considering this a collection of mineralogical and geological specimens, brought together from different sections of country by the waters, and deposited here, to illustrate the physical constitution and character of the country. This idea had no sooner occurred, than I began selecting individual pieces of it for examination, and soon had arranged on the shore a cabinet of river pebbles, which it may be curious and amusing to describe.

No. 1. Was a spheroidal pebble of common quartz; colour, grayish white, semi-transparent, and hydrogenous.

No. 2. A rounded mass of carbonate of lime; (compact secondary limestone;) colour, smoke gray; fracture, fine earthy.

No. 3. A similar water-worn mass, with a vein of calcareous spar.

No. 4. A pear-shaped pebble of common jasper; colour, a uniform chestnut brown; fracture, conchoidal; hardness, a little inferior to quartz.

No. 5. Granular quartz, rounded by attrition; colour, grayish white; easily crushed between two stones, and falling into fine semi-transparent grains.

No. 6. Hexagonal prism of rock crystal, the angles nearly obliterated by attrition.

No. 7. Rounded fragment of sand-stone; colour yellowish and reddish white; probably referable to the secondary class of rocks.

No. 8. Argillaceous pebble; colour brownish red; easily scratched with a knife.

No. 9. Smooth arguled fragment of red granite.

No. 10. Shiver of horn-stone; colour, bluish grey, translucent, and giving fire with steel.

No. 11. Egg-shaped nodule of flint, enveloped by a hard white silico-calcareous matter; colour, yellowish gray, cloudy, semi-transparent, and readily giving sparks with steel.

No. 12. Common jasper; colour, yellowish brown, veined with yellowish white, and harder than quartz.

No. 13. Tabular fragment of compact lime-stone, with an impression of the Turbinite.

Of these the rock crystal was merely accidental, the calcareous spar and flint very rare, the quartz, sand-stone, and granite, less rare, and the jasper and lime-stone very abundant. Other substances probably exist, and I noticed several species of stone, either calcareous or flinty, so disguised with ferruginous colouring, and other matter, that they were not referable by the eye to any particular species, but may be considered rather as ill-characterized varieties of both these rocks. No indurated clay, or pudding-stone, so common to other western streams; slate, particles of mica, or petrified wood, were noticed, from which it may naturally be concluded that clay-beds are not common on the river; that it yields neither mica or slate, and that the waters are not endued with the properties necessary to petrifaction. The absence also of green-stone, mica-slate, sienite [syenite], gneiss, &c. in the country in which the river originates, may hence be inferred; and, in fine, from the collection above described, one would be apt to imagine, without knowing that it actually is so, that the river is made up of streams which traverse, for the most part, a rocky region. This is actually the fact; for although there are very rich bodies of alluvial lands along the immediate margin of White River, and some of its tributaries, yet they are not very extensive, and the country is, generally speaking, a stony region.

Here, then, mineralogical science presents a new standard by which the character and fertility of an unexplored country may be with general accuracy determined, by the examination of the stony products brought down by its rivers. At least, some very useful hints may thus be gathered, and there appears no good reason why a reliance should not be placed upon information thus obtained. It is only judging of a country by samples of its earths and stones brought together by the spontaneous operations of water instead of the hands of man; and in this light the banks of a river, near its mouth, may be considered an abstract of the mineral physiognomy of the land in which it originates.

Having descended along the shore of the river a considerable distance, I now determined to return through the forest, and along the mountain-bluffs which bound the valley at the distance of half-a-mile, and descending them toward the east, join my companion at the mouth of the North Fork before dark. One of the most conspicuous objects among the trees and vegetables which skirt the banks of the river, is the sycamore, *(platanus occidentalis,)* rearing its lofty branches into the air, and distinguished from other forest-trees by its white bark and enormous size. This tree delights to grow on the immediate margin of the river, and overhangs the water's edge on both sides, but is never found to grow in the back part of the forest toward the bluffs, unless there happens to be a pond of water or a small lake there, in which case it is seen skirting its margin all around. So remarkable a fact cannot escape a person of the least observation who descends this river, or indeed any other river in the western states, whose banks are noted for rich alluvial soil, as the Ohio, the Mississippi, Illinois, Wabash, &c. It is never seen on a sterile, or dry soil; on the contrary, it may be considered as the margin-tree of the most recent, moist, black, river alluvion; and the appearance of the one is always a sure indication of the other. Very often it is hollow. This is the same tree called button-wood on the other side of the mountains, (the Alleghanies.) Another vegetable, scarcely less conspicuous, and occupying a similar soil and situation, in the latitude in which it grows, is the reed, called cane in this region, and which I take to be the *cinna arundinacea* of botanists. This plant is common to all the streams of the valley of the Mississippi below the 38 deg. of north latitude, and is first noticed on descending the Ohio, about the falls. These two species skirt the banks of this river from its largest and most remote northern tributary, as high as we have been on James' river thus far, and probably continue to the Mississippi. The other forest-trees and plants noticed at this place, and which may be set down as composing the forests of White River generally, are the following:—

Cotton-wood, *(populus angulata;)* white elm, *(ulmus Americana;)* red elm, *(ulmus fulva;)* buckeye, *(œscuius hippocastanum;)* black walnut, *(juglans nigra;)* white walnut, *(juglans tomentosa;)* white ash, *(fraxinus acuminata;)* swamp-ash, *(fraxinus juglandifolia;)* white oak, *(quercus alba;)* red oak, *(quercus rubra;)* sugar maple, *(acer saccharinum;)* mulberry, *(callicarpa Americana;)* dogwood, *(cornus florida;)* sassafras, *(laurus sassafras;)* persimmon, *(diospyros virginiana.)*

To these the valleys will add spice-wood, papaw, wild cherry, hemlock, several species of grapes, the wild pea, &c.; and the bluffs and high-lands, white and yellow pine, mountain-ash, post-oak, and cedar. The wild hop is also indigenous to the river alluvion, and the crab-apple, red plumb, and black haw, upon the plains. Many others might be added, but these are the most conspicuous on passing through a White River forest, and such as would readily attract the eye. As I approached the foot of the bluffs, vegetation became more scanty; in my ascent, at the height of one hundred feet above the forest level, the rocks were entirely naked, presenting an almost perpendicular wall to the river, but the summit was covered by yellow pine and cedar, sustained by a deposite of oceanic alluvion. The height of this

Cedar glade with exposed bedrock, near Bull Shoals, Arkansas, 1993.
PHOTOGRAPH BY MILTON RAFFERTY.

bluff may be estimated at three hundred feet above the water. It runs parallel with the river, at the distance of from a quarter to half-a-mile, and is much
broken and interrupted by lateral valleys and streams. It is uniformly, so far
as could be examined without the labour of digging and clearing away the
rubbish at its base, a mass of stratified secondary limestone, with impressions of univalve shells near its summit. On my descent I was surprised to
observe, about half-way down, very large angular masses of common white
quartz, resting upon the tabular rocks of carbonate of lime, and manifestly
out of place. Being discoloured externally by the weather, and by atmos-
pheric dust and moss, I at first mistook these rocks for lime-stone; but on
hammering off several corners, perceived them to be quartz. This set me
looking sharply round to discover some primitive strata from which they
might have been detached, but I was unable to detect any, and I must leave
the phenomenon unexplained.

That small pieces of quartz rock should have been detached from primitive strata in distant parts of the country, and deposited upon secondary
lime-stone with other alluvial matter by water, excites no surprise, even if
the masses weigh a ton, or more; but to see masses of the size of a common
house, presenting angles of fourteen to twenty feet, and probably weighing
an hundred tons a piece, is certainly extraordinary, and does not admit of a
ready explanation upon any principle of alluvial deposits now taught. They
could not have fallen from the mountainous heights above, for those heights
are composed of shell lime-stone. Have these masses of quartz been ejected
by volcanic fire, or is it possible that any power of water could have upborne
them to the elevated heights they now occupy?

SATURDAY, JAN. 16TH.

On returning from the woods yesterday, the hunters had not yet arrived with
our canoe, but made their appearance at dusk, accompanied by several
neighbours and friends in their canoes, who also came down to trade, making a party of twelve or fourteen in all. Whisky soon began to circulate freely,
and by the time they had unloaded their canoes, we began plainly to discover that a scene of riot and drinking was to follow. Of all this, we were destined to be unwilling witnesses; for as there was but one house, and that a
very small one, necessity compelled us to pass the night together; but sleep
was not to be obtained. Every mouth, hand, and foot, were in motion. Some
drank, some sang, some danced, a considerable proportion attempted all

Calico Rock and the White River, 1994. PHOTOGRAPH BY MILTON RAFFERTY.

three together, and a scene of undistinguishable bawling and riot ensued. An occasional quarrel gave variety to the scene, and now and then, one drunker than the rest, fell sprawling upon the floor, and for a while remained quiet. We alone remained listeners to this grand exhibition of human noises, beastly intoxication, and mental and physical nastiness. We did not lie down to sleep, for that was dangerous. Thus the night rolled heavily on, and as soon as light could be discerned in the morning we joyfully embarked in our canoe, happy in having escaped bodily disfiguration, and leaving such as could yet stand, vociferating with all their might like some delirious man upon his dying bed, who makes one desperate effort to arise, and then falls back in death.

Half-a-mile below Matney's, we passed the mouth of the Great North Fork, a stream which we had followed down, to within ten miles of its mouth, as detailed in the former part of this journal. Six miles below, we passed a swift run of water in the river called the Crooked Rapids. They are no wise dangerous or difficult to be passed.

Ten miles more brought us in sight of the Calico Rock, a noted bluff in a sudden bend of the river. It is one of those rare and fanciful works of nature which are seldom met with, and is approached under circumstances well calculated to heighten the effect of a scene in itself very striking and picturesque. On turning a bend in the river, suddenly the rock appears before you at the distance of 600 yards, and seems, as you glide toward it, to present a barrier to the progress of the river. It is a lofty smooth wall of stratified lime-stone rock, presenting a diversity of colour in squares, stripes, spots, or angles, all confusedly mixed and arranged according to the inimitable pencil of nature, and hence its name. People tell you, that all kinds of rocks are here to be found, and an opinion is prevalent that metallic substances of great value exist in these rocks. The deception is naturally created, and readily believed in by those who only look upon the surface of things; but a little examination shows the fallacy of appearances. Instead of being composed of many rocks differing in their component parts, it is one rock of the same substance, and internally of the same colour and texture, namely, floet lime-stone. This is overlayed by a stratum of ochery clay, and red and greenish coloured earths, full of ferruginous particles, which have been washed by rains into the crevices of the horizontal strata of stone, and thence oozing down the surface, have communicated to it different colours. These have been in some degree altered, variegated, or set by the acids and juices of oak and other leaves: also extracted by rains, giving to the surface of the rock a singular appearance, of what the German mineralogists, with peculiar significancy, term *angelaufenen farben,* (tarnished colours). Fourteen miles below the Calico Rock we stopped for the night, on the left bank of the river, at Jeffery's, having canoed thirty miles.

SUNDAY, JAN. 17TH.

On descending five miles, we stopped at a Mr. Williams's to prepare breakfast. Here some hunters were gathering to hear an itinerant preacher. Thirty miles below, we stopped for the night at widow Lafferty's, on the right bank of the river. Some excitement prevails among the people occupying the right bank of White River, on account of the recent treaty concluded with the Cherokee Indians. By it those Indians relinquish certain tracts of land in the state of Tennessee, but are to receive in exchange the lands lying between the north bank of the Arkansaw, and the south bank of White River. Those people, therefore, who have located themselves upon the right bank of the river, and improved farms, are now necessitated to relinquish them, which is considered a piece of injustice.

Monday, Jan. 18th.

Much had been said along the river, respecting a tin mine reported to exist on the north bank of the river in this vicinity, and although not prepared to find this metal among secondary rocks, I had determined to make it a point of particular inquiry, and after descending the river five miles this morning, stopped about the hour of breakfast, at the house of the person (Mr. Jones,) on whose lands the discovery was reported to have been made. He confirmed all we had heard on the subject; said that a very large body of singular ore, supposed to be tin, had been found some eight or ten miles north of his house, on the high-lands; that it lay in a valley upon the surface of the earth, upon a kind of rotten lime-stone rock, with a small stream running by, &c. He now produced some lumps of the ore. It was a species of the mountain iron-ore (iron glance,) of a bluish gray colour, great weight, and possessed considerable metallic lustre; destitute, however, of those tarnished colours which serve to beautify the surface of certain varieties of specular iron glance. This incident seems to show how readily persons who have devoted little attention to the subject, are deceived in the appearances of a mineral, and how prone they are to ascribe to it a value which it does not possess.

At the distance of fifteen miles below Jones's, we passed Hardin's Ferry; dwelling-house on the south bank. Here the main road from Missouri to Arkansaw crosses the river, and a mail is carried from St. Louis to the post of Arkansaw, (now the seat of Territorial Government, March 1820,) once a month. Two miles below is Morrison's Ferry, a branch of the same road crossing there, and eight miles farther Poke Bayou [Batesville], a village of a dozen houses, situated on the north bank of the river, where we arrived at about four o'clock in the afternoon, and were entertained with hospitality by Mr. Robert Bean, merchant of that place.

A gradual change in the face of the country for the last thirty miles, before reaching this spot, is observable. The bottom lands, as you descend, increase in width; the bluffs become more remote, and decrease in height, and finally disappear a few miles above Hardin's Ferry, where that extensive alluvial formation, which reaches to the banks of the Mississippi, commences. From this fork, the scenery is unvaried. A rich level plain, covered with heavy forest-trees and canebrake, extends as far as the eye can reach, on both banks of the river, gradually depressed toward the Mississippi, where it is subject to semi-annual inundation. At this place, the banks are elevated thirty feet above the present level of the water, and are subject to falling in during the high spring and autumnal floods. In other respects, the situation of Poke Bayou is pleasant, and advantageous as a commercial and agricultural depôt. Here we concluded to quit the river, and pursue the Arkansaw road, on foot, through Lawrence, Cape Girardeau, Wayne, and Madison counties, toward Potosi. As a preparatory step, we have disposed of our canoe, skins, &c. and provided ourselves with travelling knapsacks.

VI

From Poke Bayou to Potosi

TUESDAY, JAN. 19TH.

Before leaving the banks of White River, it is due to the hardy, frank, and independent hunters, through whose territories we have travelled, and with whom we have from time to time sojourned, to say, that we have been uniformly received at their cabins with a blunt welcome, and experienced the most hospitable and generous treatment. This conduct, which we were not prepared to expect, is the more remarkable, in being wholly disinterested, for no remuneration in money for such entertainment (with a very few exceptions,) was ever demanded; but, when presented, uniformly refused, on the principle of its not being customary to accept pay of the traveller, for any thing necessary to his sustenance. Nor can we quit the house at which we have been made to feel our return to the land of civilization, after an absence of several months, without a grateful expression of our sense of the kind civilities and generous attention with which we have been treated. There is but one thing I have to regret on my departure from Poke Bayou; it is my inability to carry along my entire collections in natural history, too bulky and too heavy to be conveyed in a shoulder pack, the only mode of transportation at our command. Selecting, however, such as were most rare or interesting, either from locality, or physical constitution, I filled my pack to a point, which, superadded to the weight of a gun, rifle, pouch, portfolio, &c. I judged myself capable of carrying; and we left Poke Bayou at ten o'clock, taking the high-road toward the north-west. For the first five miles we passed across the alluvial tract, extending northwardly to the river, on which several farms and plantations are located, and the country wears a look of agricultural industry and increasing population. The farms, the improvements upon them, and the road we travelled, all appeared new. The houses were constructed of logs, and the lands fenced with rails laid in the zig-zag manner practised in western Virginia and Kentucky. We now entered on the secondary lime-stone formation, which bounds the Mississippi alluvion on the west, a tract of country gently elevated, covered with a flinty soil and scanty vegetation, and indented by innumerable little valleys, which give it a rough and barren aspect. On this are found no settlements in the distance of thirteen miles, during the last mile of which I had wrenched my ancle in such a way as to render it extremely painful in walking, and we stopped early in the afternoon, at a small plantation fortuitously at hand.

WEDNESDAY, JAN. 20TH.

An application of dissolved muriate of soda and flannels, surcharged with microcosmic salts in natural solution, did little to mitigate the swelling of my foot; and, after a night passed in sleepless anxiety, I arose without feeling any sensible diminution of pain, and without the ability to continue the journey on foot. This accident could not have happened at a spot where medical aid, or the conveniency of transportation, was in all probability more completely out of reach, and one of the most unpleasant delays threatened to ensue. Here chance supplied, as it frequently happens, what could not have been procured in any other way. A traveller passing on horseback agreed, for a trifling compensation, to let me ride his horse to the banks of the south fork of Strawberry River, while he himself performed the journey on foot. This helped me twelve miles, and we arrived about noon. The road lay across an uninhabited tract, much cut up by little valleys, worn out of shelly limestone, and covered with a stratum of gravelly clay, bearing post oaks and black oaks. A mile before reaching the river we entered upon an alluvial plain, which continued to the village seated upon its margin. Here were fifteen buildings, scattered along the banks of the stream, including a small grist-mill turned by water, a whisky-distillery, a black-smith's-shop, and a tavern. Feeling somewhat relieved, I concluded to hobble on four miles farther to the main stream of the river, where we arrived before night, and stopped at a farmer's house, my foot having in the meanwhile become exceedingly painful.

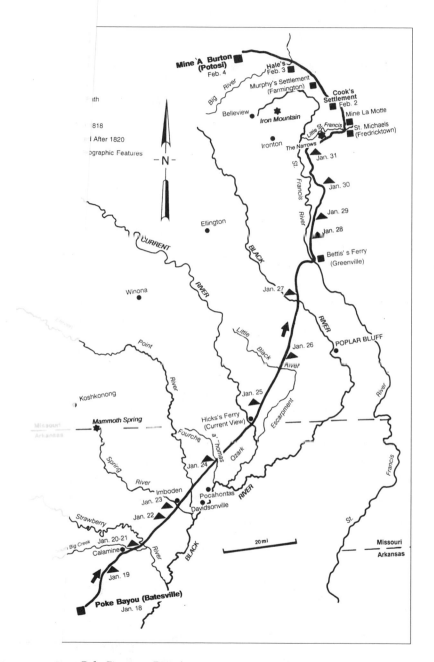

Mine `A Burton
(Potosi)
Feb. 4

Hale's
Feb. 3

Murphy's Settlement
(Farmington)

Cook's
Settlement
Feb. 2

Big River

Belleview

Iron Mountain

Mine La Motte

St. Francis

St. Michaels
(Fredricktown)

Ironton

The Narrows

Little St.

Jan. 31

Jan. 30

St. Francis River

Jan. 29

Jan. 28

Ellington

BLACK

Bettis's Ferry
(Greenville)

CURRENT

Jan. 27

RIVER

RIVER

POPLAR BLUFF

Winona

Jan. 26

Point

Little

Koshkonong

River

Black

River

Jan. 25

Mammoth Spring

Hicks's Ferry
(Current View)

Escarpment

Missouri
Arkansas

Fourche

a`Thomas

Ozark

Spring

Jan. 24

Francis

River

Imboden
Jan. 23

Pocahontas

RIVER

St.

Davidsonville

Strawberry

Jan. 22

20 mi

Missouri
Arkansas

Big Creek

Jan. 20-21

Calamine

River

BLACK

Jan. 19

Poke Bayou (Batesville)
Jan. 18

ith

818

After 1820

ographic Features

—N—

The route from Poke Bayou to Potosi. CARTOGRAPHY BY HEATHER CONLEY.

THURSDAY, JAN. 21ST.

It was in vain to attempt travelling under such circumstances. I determined to halt, and await the recovery of my foot, while Mr. Pettibone, anxious to terminate a journey which had already been protracted to an unexpected length, concluded to proceed alone toward St. Louis; and we parted at nine o'clock, after having mutually shared the inconveniences of a pedestrian journey through the woods for seventy-five days.

FRIDAY, JAN. 22D.

Left alone, my impatience of delay increased, and I lost the benefit of no application which circumstances, diligence, or the united skill of my hostess and myself could supply. Forty-one hours thus devoted, superadded to the advantages of rest, abated the swelling of my ancle, and enabled me without great inconvenience to walk. I determined, therefore, to proceed by easy stages for several days, until it became sufficiently invigorated to permit a bolder step, and crossed the Strawberry River this morning at nine. Proceeding with an easy pace, and by frequent resting, I gained ten miles by night, and stopped at the Dogwood Spring, a noted resting-place on the dividing ridge between Strawberry and Spring Rivers, named in allusion to the *cornus florida,* abundant there. The alluvial soil continued two miles beyond the banks of Strawberry, and for that distance improved farms and dwellings skirted the road; then commenced a calcareous ridge, undulated by valleys running parallel to the general course of the rivers, sterile in appearance, and wholly without improvements. On every declivity the strata of secondary rock were exposed to view. Within five miles of the Dogwood Spring I passed a large body of vitreous iron ore, (the brown hæmatite [hematite] of mineralogists,) on descending a hill on the right side of the road. It lies scattered over the surface of the earth for many acres.

SATURDAY, JAN. 23D.

Ten miles beyond this brought me to the banks of Spring River, a large and beautiful stream, which originates in one large spring forty miles above, and, after receiving the river Elevenpoints [Eleven Point River], unites with Black River ten miles below. It is a clear stream, and affords considerable bodies of choice intervale. A mile before reaching it the alluvial soil commences.

Here Indian corn, wheat, rye, oats, cotton, and tobacco, all flourish in the same field.

SUNDAY, JAN. 24TH.

I was carried across the river in a canoe. A mile beyond, the river bottom terminates, and I ascended the calcareous ridge of secondary rock which separates its waters from those of Elevenpoints. Neither the soil, the vegetation, nor geological character of the country, present any variations entitled to notice. At twelve o'clock I reached the banks of Elevenpoints, and was ferried over in a canoe. This stream is nearly as large as Spring River with which it unites three miles above its junction with Big Black River. Its waters are beautifully clear, and it affords a strip of alluvion a mile across from hill to hill.

Davidsonville, the seat of justice of Lawrence county, is situated seven miles eastwardly, on the point of land formed by the junction of Spring with Black River. It unites the advantages of an uninterrupted water-communication through White River with the Mississippi, and through that with the ocean, but is a place of little note or importance at present. Half a mile beyond the north bank of the Elevenpoints, the ridge of secondary calcareous rock, separating its valley from that of Fourche à Thomas [Fourche River], is struck, and the road winds along through a sterile and uninhabited country for nine miles. On one of the highest elevations of this intervening ridge, and equi-distant from both streams, I passed a bed of black oxide of manganese. It possesses little weight, is earthy, and soils the finger like soot. Some red oxide is in combination. The quantity is immense. As day-light withdrew, I entered the valley of Fourche à Thomas, having travelled nineteen miles.

MONDAY, JAN. 25TH.

Fourche à Thomas is a stream of lesser size than either Strawberry or Elevenpoints; it affords, however, some excellent lands, and the alluvial formation, though not extensive, is very rich, and several large and well-improved farms decorate its valley. It originates in high-lands forty miles west, and unites with Black River, after winding a course of fifty miles. Settlements continue to the north of this stream six miles, and the ridge of high-lands by which it is divided from the Currents River, is less elevated, less rocky, better wooded, and better calculated for agriculture, than those already mentioned. The distance, therefore, between these two streams, which is sixteen miles, appears less to the foot-traveller on that account, as there is more to occupy the eye, and less to weary the feet; for while we are viewing plantations, and the habitations of man occasionally interspersed among the woods, the time and the distance pass imperceptibly away, but the unvaried barrenness of the wilderness is tiresome. The eye seizes with avidity any new object which promises variety, and this variety is ever more pleasing when associated with the idea of being useful, and capable in some way of promoting the happiness, or subserving the economy of human life. The rock strata, where apparent, are calcareous, and secondary. The *quercus tinctoria* is the most common tree. Two miles before reaching the Currents, the river alluvion commences. Its fructuferous qualities are at once recognised by the unusual size of the trees, cane, and shrubbery, by which it is covered. At three o'clock I reached the banks of the river at Hicks' Ferry [Current View], and was conveyed over in a ferry-flat, or scow. This is the fifth river I have passed since leaving Poke Bayou, in a short distance of ninety miles, all running parallel with each other from west to east, separated by similar ridges of calcareous rock, having analogous alluvions on their banks, and all discharging their waters into Black River, which, like an artificial drain, runs nearly from north to south, and, catching their waters, conveys them through White River into the Mississippi. That singular stream, which itself preserves an exact parallelism with the Mississippi during its whole course, is not less remarkable for the number of streams it receives from the west, than for receiving no tributary of any magnitude in its whole course from the east. This is owing to a singular configuration of the country, the examination of which would, perhaps, prove very interesting to the geologist as well as the geographer, and possibly throw some new light on the subject of alluvial deposits, the circumstances under which they have been formed, their relative ages, and other contemporaneous matters, which have not received a proper degree of consideration. The lack of tributaries from the east bank of Black River, results from the alluvial tract extending from its eastern bank to the western bank of the Mississippi, and which has a gradual descent from the former to the latter, draining off the waters even from within 100 yards of its banks. On the west it is successively swelled, as you traverse the country from White River northward, by Strawberry, Spring River, Elevenpoints, Fourche à Thomas, and the Currents, all streams of considerable magnitude, and entitled to the particular notice of the future geographers of Missouri and Arkansaw. Of these, the Fourche à Thomas is the smallest, and the

Currents by far the largest. The latter is, indeed, a noble stream. It is 1,000 feet wide at the Ferry, and has an average depth of eight feet. It originates in springs in the Missouri barrens, 250 miles west, and affords, in its whole length, bodies of alluvial lands well worthy the attention of the planter and speculator. Its sources are amidst bluffs of secondary limestone, which are extremely cavernous, and afford saltpetre. Our residence for several days in one of these caves, while passing through these regions in the month of November of the last year, has already been detailed in a former part of this journal. At Hicks's Ferry, a town [Current View] is in contemplation. The site is dry, airy, and eligible, and will command many advantages for mercantile purposes. A mile and a half north, the alluvial tract is succeeded by secondary limestone, rising in elevated ridges, which serve to separate the valley of Currents from that of Little Black River. Here night approached, and I stopped six miles north of the Currents, at a farmer's house that happend to be contiguous, having performed a journey of twenty-three miles.

TUESDAY, JAN. 26TH.

Thirteen miles beyond this, I entered the valley of Little Black River, a stream of clear water ninety feet wide, with a swift current. This is the principal south branch of Black River, and joins the main stream seven miles below. The alluvion on its banks is not extensive. Some improvements are however made, and the newness of the buildings, fences, and clearings, indicate here, as at every other inhabited part of the road for the last 100 miles, a recent and augmenting population. This is chiefly composed of emigrants from Pennsylvania, the Carolinas, Kentucky, and Tennessee. Two miles north of Little Black River I halted for the night, at an early hour, my foot giving symptoms of returning lameness. Distance fifteen miles.

WEDNESDAY, JAN. 27TH.

The ensuing sixteen miles brought me to the banks of Big Black River, a large and rapid stream, being the seventh river crossed in a distance of 130 miles; and all of which are ultimately united in this. I was ferried over in a canoe, and lodged a mile beyond, at a house seated at the intermediate points, where the river alluvion is terminated by calcareous rock. I here found myself in Wayne county, according to a late division of Lawrence, by the territorial legislature of Missouri. Agriculture forms the principal employment of the inhabitants along this stream, and its tributaries. A small proportion are mechanics, less merchants, and very few professional men. The soil and climate are considered favourable for the different species of our domesticated graminea. Wheat and corn are the surest, and most advantageous crops. Rye, oats, flax, and tobacco, are also cultivated, the latter partially; and cotton is also grown, but not as a market crop, merely for family convenience, and domestic consumption. The raising of cattle has also engrossed considerable attention in this section of country, and graziers have been well remunerated. St. Louis, St. Genevieve, Kaskaskia, and other distant markets, have drawn a part of their supplies from this quarter. This business, which was very inviting at first, having been carried to excess, has produced a natural re-action, and it is not now considered an object to drive their stock to remote markets.

THURSDAY, JAN. 28TH.

The road from Black River to the river St. Francis, a distance of seventeen miles, lies for the first eight miles across an elevated ridge of secondary limestone rock, intersected by deep valleys, running in all directions, which give it somewhat the appearance of a plain full of high conical hills. These are covered with a stony soil that sustains a growth of yellow pine. The remainder of the road is carried along a gravelly, dry valley, that winds among similar bluffs to the river, and there terminates in the alluvial formation of the St. Francis. Here is a village of ten or fifteen houses, including a grist-mill; and a public ferry is kept by Dr. Bettis. The St. Francis is a large steam, and waters a great extent of country. Its length is stated at 500 miles; near its head are situated the valuable lead-mines of La Motte, and the iron mountain of Bellevieu is situated on its principal south-western branch. Toward its junction with the Mississippi, the lands are low and overflowed. The greater part of the fine rich alluvial margin of this stream is, however, susceptible of successful cultivation, and it is already the seat of one of the most rich and populous agricultural settlements in the territory. I crossed the ferry at Battis' [*sic*] at three o'clock, and lodged six miles beyond, on the road to St. Michael's, having travelled twenty-three miles. I have this day observed the *hamamelis virginica* in blossom.

FRIDAY, JAN. 29TH.

I was on the road toward St. Michael this morning before day-light. After travelling a mile, it commenced raining, and poured down incessantly, until

I reached the next house, being seven miles. There, as the rain continued, I remained until the next day.

SATURDAY, JAN. 30TH.

The rain continued with extraordinary violence during the greater part of the night. The morning was cloudy and unsettled. I proceeded twenty miles, and lodged near the bank of the St. Francis, on the road toward Bellevieu. A vast quantity of water had fallen upon the earth, and the streams were swollen to an unusual height. Every small brook was increased to a torrent, and channels dry at ordinary seasons were now filled with water. The earth, also, was completely surcharged, and wherever it consisted of alluvion, deep mud was the consequence. This rendered travelling very fatiguing. On proceeding five miles along the main road, the country became very rough and barren, and here blocks of granite were found, reposing promiscuously upon secondary lime-stone. These fragments of primitive rock, at first scattering, soon became abundant, and in the course of the succeeding mile I found myself in a region of granite. Here the country bore a very rugged aspect, and the road wound about among piles and hills of granite rock, in which no stratification, and no order of arrangement, could be observed. This is the older red granite of geologists, consisting chiefly of flesh-coloured feldspar mixed with quartz, and a very little mica, the former ingredient, however, predominating. It extends about twenty miles north-westwardly, and has a breadth of about six or eight, being surrounded on all sides by secondary rocks, and is at once the most singular and interesting object in the geological character of the whole valley of the Mississippi, so far as yet discovered. So considerable a body of primitive rock, in the midst of so unparalleled an extent of secondary strata, furnishes an interesting subject of inquiry, and its occurrence is certainly without a parallel in the scientific annals of our country. Its geognostic situation is, however, readily explained by either of the theories at present taught; but whether this mass of granite is the peak of a pre-existing mountain, around which the calcareous rock has subsequently been deposited, or whether since upheaved by volcanic fire, will admit of some doubt. The existence of blocks of granite, reposing upon calcareous rock, a mile distant from the main body, and where nothing short of a volcanic power appears capable of having thrown or conveyed them, seems to favour the latter hypothesis.

SUNDAY, JAN. 31ST.

The weather continued cloudy and unsettled. On reaching the ford of the St. Francis I found the river so flooded by the late rains, that it was impossible to cross without a canoe, and this was wanting. Thus defeated in my intention of visiting the Iron mountain, and the granite ridges of Bellevieu, I pursued up the banks of the north-eastern branch of the river, through a populous settlement, for a distance of ten miles, and passed the night at a planter's, four miles below St. Michael [Fredricktown]. The granitic rock has been constantly in view.

MONDAY, FEB. 1.

I advanced but three miles this day. During the morning it rained, and continued, with occasional cessations, until night. Much had been told me of the natural appearances of the Narrows, where the river is compressed between lofty hills of granite, and of the shaking of the earth, sometimes experienced there. It is seldom that these relations of the country people are entitled to any credit, and my own experience abundantly satisfies me, that the traveller who turns out of his way to see surprising things, on no better authority, is often sent on a fool's errand. I was disappointed, therefore, to find the Narrows of St. Francis well worthy of a visit. Here the river, narrowed to half its width, forces itself between two elevated ridges of red granite, and brawling over its rugged bed, pitches, at successive leaps, twenty or thirty feet in the distance of half a mile. These ridges rise to a height of six or seven hundred feet, and are capped with oak-trees, except on the sides facing the river, where the rock, during the lapse of ages, fallen off, and the fragments rolling downwards, so accumulated as to give the ridges the appearance of two mighty and confused piles of granitic stones. No signs of vegetable life are found upon them. At the water's edge, there is a vein of micaceous iron ore, which is considered silver by the neighbouring people. Some blocks of greenstone porphyry are also seen among these interesting mineral ruins. Radiated quartz, iron pyrites, and a species of massive mountain iron ore, are also the production of this region. The contiguous calcareous strata on the east afford galena and blende. During that remarkable series of earthquakes which this country, in common with all the valley of the Mississippi, experienced in December, 1811, and which continued with intermissions until 1813, large masses of granite rock were shook from these

Aerial view of the Narrows of the Little St. Francis River, 1995.
PHOTOGRAPH BY MILTON RAFFERTY.

heights, and precipitated into the valley of the St. Francis. The effects of these dreadful earthquakes are still visible in many parts of Missouri and Arkansaw, but the most striking alterations were made in the alluvial district of New-Madrid county, the capital of which was, in part, precipitated into the Mississippi, and the natural physiognomy of that country is much disfigured by eruptions and by lakes. It is even added, that a tremulous motion of the earth is still sometimes observable in that section of country. The most interesting, and, indeed, the only condensed body of facts, relative to these earthquakes, which is to be found among the literary papers of the United States, were collected and published by Dr. Samuel L. Mitchill, in the *first volume of the Transactions of the Literary and Philosophical Society of New-York.*

TUESDAY, FEB. 2D.

I determined to make another attempt to cross into Bellevieu by the upper ford of the St. Francis; but here also I found the water too deep, and was compelled to pursue the more circuitous route through St. Genevieve county. A mile's travelling brought me into St. Michael, a village of sixty houses, and the county seat of Madison, according to a recent act of the legislature. It has three stores and a post-office. This village was originally settled by the French, and has for many years been in a state of decline; but since its selection as the seat of justice for the new county, has received what is called *a start,* that is, has rapidly improved in appearance. Here a road diverges to St. Genevieve, which is situated thirty miles east on the banks of the Mississippi. Two miles beyond St. Michael, on the road toward St. Louis, we pass the lead-mines of La Motte [Mine La Motte]. The road runs among the excavations, which are very numerous, and cover a great extent of country. The ore worked is a sulphuret; it is found reposing in beds in alluvial soil, without any matrix. The rock strata here are calcareous: two miles south-west commences the tract of insular granite. These mines have been worked with little interruption for a century, and are not yet exhausted; but, on the contrary, yield as much metal as formerly. Large piles of the ore, crystallized in shining facets, were lying near the road as I passed, and a number of workmen engaged either in the excavations, or smelting. Nine miles beyond the mines, the traveller enters Cook's settlement, a fine district of land in the interior of St. Genevieve county, with a rapidly increasing population. Here I reposed for the night.

WEDNESDAY, FEB. 3D.

A tract of oceanic alluvion extends from this to the banks of Big River, a distance of twenty miles, in the course of which a number of plantations are passed, but the country is susceptible of more extensive improvements, and will, no doubt, in a short time, attract a portion of that emigration which is now flowing into all parts of the valley of the Mississippi and the Missouri. Murphy's settlement [Farmington], at the distance of eight miles beyond Cook's, is already a large and flourishing neighbourhood of industrious farmers, and presents many well-cultivated fields, fenced in a neat and substantial manner, with young apple and peach-orchards, and framed dwelling-houses, clap-boarded in the eastern style. There is also a post-office in this settlement, where a mail is received once a-week, a school-house, and a physician resident. All these things indicate the wealth, the industry, and the intelligence of the inhabitants.

Between Murphy's settlement and Big River, there are no settlements. As you approach the banks of the latter, the lands gradually descend, and terminate in a very rich river alluvion. Its width is nearly a mile from hill to hill, and it is the seat of numerous plantations and well-cultivated farms, where large quantities of wheat and corn are raised. A great proportion of the former is floured for exportation, and of the latter, distilled for the same purpose. This river describes in its course the form of a horse-shoe around the extensive lead-mines of Washington county, in the centre of which stands its capital, Potosi, and affords some facilities to the transportation of goods. It originates on table lands, which separate its waters from those of the St. Francis, and forms a junction with the Merrimack thirty miles above the confluence of that river with the Mississippi. Near the head of Big River are situated some of the most extensive and valuable iron-mines, though not worked, in America, and the calcareous rocks bordering its banks are decidedly the most metalliferous strata, in ores of lead, which the United States, or any mining district of Europe or America affords.

Thursday, Feb. 1th.

From this spot, (Hale's on Big River,) [Desloge] the roads diverge eastwardly to St. Genevieve, northwardly to Herculaneum and St. Louis, and westwardly to Potosi, which is situated at a distance of fifteen miles. Toward this I hastened with a buoyancy of spirit, consequent upon the reflection that the termination of my journey was at hand. After crossing the ford, and the alluvial bottoms extending westwardly from the river, the road winds up a succession of elevated hills for the distance of three of four miles. Here commences a sterile plain, indented with gentle valleys, watered by innumerable rivulets, and covered with a very uniform growth of black oaks and post oaks, and in the summer season by a vigorous undergrowth of wild grass, flowers, and vines. The soil is a deep stratum of red marly clay, interspersed with shivers of horn-stone and jasper, radiated quartz, and heavy spar. These evidences of the existence of lead-ore in the earth denoted my approach to Potosi, where I arrived at three o'clock in the afternoon, after an absence of ninety days, and having travelled more than nine hundred miles.

TRANSALLEGANIA,

OR

THE GROANS OF MISSOURI.

a Poem.

BY H. R. SCHOOLCRAFT.

"The things we know are rich and rare,
But how the devil came they there?"
POPE'S LETTERS.

When wilds that were lately the panther's retreat,
Were turned to plantations and covered with wheat;
When emigrants thickened, and congress debates,
Turned full on the west, and they cut off new states;
The king of the metals, (who deep, under ground,
Reposed with his subjects in slumber profound,)
Alarm'd by the tumult he heard on the earth,
From Mexico travelled in haste to the north;
Nor paused he for river, or mountain, or plain,
Till he reached the frontiers of his golden domain;
There stopped on a mountain, all reeking with heat,
(The Arkansaw winding along at his feet,)
And surveyed with amazement the torrent that prest—
The stream of migration that rolled to the west.
From mountain to mountain a prospect he takes—
From the gulph on the south to the northern lakes,
And all the wide scene, valley, hillock, and glen,
Resounds with the tumult of business and men:
They are driving the savage before them amain,
And people each forest, and culture each plain.
He sees how they struggle with fortune and fate,
How toil to be happy, and pant to be great:
He hears the axe sounding on every hill,
And the woods are re-echoing liberty's thrill:
All countries and climates, "the bond and the free,"
To people the wilderness closely agree,
From Maine's rocky borders the emigrants pour,
And are leaving the fruitful Connecticut's shore,
The Hudson, Potomac, and Delaware, sigh,
For friends who had quit them, they hardly knew why;
The exiles of Europe, the poor, the oppress'd,
All, all, they are bending their steps to the west.
One object impels them, one passion inspires—
The rage for improvement, for wealth the desires;
And alike in all countries, conditions, and states,
This passion is cherished, prevails and inflates;
The rich in it see an increase of estate,
And the poor are still flattered by hopes to be great.

Thus season on season new converts engage,
And support and augment the migratory rage:
Now here and now there its direction it turns,
On Wabash it kindles, on Miami burns,
And now on the fertile Scioti delights,
And now on the Washitaw fondly invites:
Still changing, each season new regions display,
No boundaries check it, no streams can allay,
No land is too distant, no climate too hot,
No forest too heavy, no stream too remote;
They move, they inhabit, they cultivate all,
And were oceans no check, would encompass the ball:
Even now they approach my extensive domain,
And Missouri already is peopled with men.

Thus the monarch discours'd, and with sorrow oppress'd,
Full many a sigh shook his glittering breast;
He thought on the woes he had brought on mankind,
In countries remote, and in ages behind;
How fatal his friendships, and yet that his hates
Had overturned empires, and founded new states.
Of Ophir he pondered, and passed in review,
His Mexican robbers, and foes in Peru;
And he sighed for his friendships so fatally dear,
And brave Montezuma recalled with a tear:
And he feared that this great, this all-conquering press,
This progress of empire, stir, business, distress,
Would not only acquire an unlimited bound,
But discover his very retreats in the ground;
That his subjects and kin would be eagerly sought,
And wofully handled, and dreadfully taught;
That they all should be dragged out with bucket and chain,
And hammered, and pounded, and melted with pain.
He knew in such tortures men take a delight,
And he dreaded a miner, and hated the light.
But while thus he debated with reason and fear,
A sudden commotion resounds in his ear;
There were horses and men in tumultuous throng,

Came tramping, and talking, and rattling along;
The farmer was ploughing in sensible view,
The woodman he chopp'd, and the blacksmith he blew;
There were lawyers and merchants, all nations and brogues,
Scotch, English, and French, Irish, Yankees, and rogues;
And a school it was building, a master was found,
And was drawing out plans and surveying the ground.
Such a tumult and toil left no reason to doubt,
That his fears were all true, and a town was laid out:
But how great was his tremor, vexation, and hate,
When "a state" was re-echoed, "Missouri, a state."

In so sad a dilemma, dejected and grave,
The monarch withdrew to his closet, a cave;
Bethinking all peaceful to take into view
The course it were proper a king should pursue.
He pondered, and plotted, in fear, and in haste,
Now gnawed on his quill, and now writ, now erased;
Alternately flagging in fear and in doubt,
Or bent on campaigning with courage devout;
Now bending his thoughts upon leaving the land,
And now on the fame of a resolute stand:
At length, now concluding his foes to harass,
He resolved to assemble his subjects *en masse:*
And appointed a time, and provided a place,
Where they all might assemble, talk, plan, and embrace.
For, quoth he, to prevent being dragged out to light,
We more can accomplish by planning, than fight;
And however the mortals on earth may deny it,
There is more to be got without fighting, than by it;
For though they gain treaties, they lose it in bones,
And such points are not valued by fossils and stones.

The monarch of metals, whose absolute sway,
Not minerals only, but mortals obey;
Wherever he journies, whatever betide,
Has always companions and slaves at his side;
And hide as he may hide, and go where he will,

Has *mica-slate, granite,* and *quartz* with him still.
Hence the king had no sooner resolved on a plan,
Than he bid them proclaim it throughout his domain:
"Tell the Metals I summon them all to this shore,
Or in person to come, or by delegate ore:
To the uttermost mines of my kingdom go haste,
Search dell, traverse mountain, explore every waste,
Let no cave be unentered, no rock unexplored,
Where metal could harbour, or oxide could hoard;
Every bank, every hill, every stone, every shore,
Search by fire and by acid, hunt over and o'er!
That all kin of my ancient and glorious line
May hear of my summons, and know my design:
Go tell them, I hail their approach with a kiss,
I study their safety, I pant for their bliss;
And I would not intrude on their solid repose,
Were it not that my enemies drive me to blows.
But be cautious, friend Granite, lest thou shouldst be seen
In thy tour by our foes, mineralogical men;
Fly the face of the earth, keep the underground wave,
By stratum, or cavity, crevice, or cave;
So our scheme shall be secret, and no body scan,
Our flinty designs on our enemy—man."

The courier mounted on mettlesome steed,
Departed full gaily, a trooper of speed;
Nor paused he for pleasure, nor stopped he for bait,
He spurred on through *limestone,* and sweated through *slate;*
He travelled through *gneiss,* where metals were in't;
He galloped through *green-stone,* and worried through *flint;*
He cantered through *gravel,* where *porphyry* lay,
And floundered through *gypsum,* and trotted through *clay;*
Nor could *sienite* stop his unparalleled course,
Though *adamant* injured the heels of his horse;
But whene'er his steed lingered, (a hint for hussars,)
He urged him to canter by pelting with spars;
For he gave him no rest for refreshment or bait,
Till he'd traversed the empire, and summoned the state:

Then for all his unkindness he promptly atones,
By feeding his horse with some beautiful stones.
A cave on the Arkansaw, spacious and dread,
The monarch had chose for the regal parade;
Where, guarded by minions, he patiently waits
The gathering council, and coming debates.

The first who attended was blue-visaged Lead,
Who had quitted Potosi in haste, as he said;
For his friends they were many, and occupied ground
For seventy leagues in the country around;
And the moment he heard of his majesty's will,
He set off with speed over dingle and hill;
And so great was his haste, and the journey so far,
Carried only one friend, it was ponderous *spar*.
Then raising his voice, though with sorrow opprest,
Thus vented the feelings that burned in his breast:
"My friends in Missouri, my kin and compeers,
All smarting with pains, and all bathed in their tears;
After many long years of oppression and grief,
At length are encouraged to try for relief:
And assembled in council from seventy mines,
I bear their commission, and speak their designs.
It is more than a century, since we were first
Discovered by mortals, discovered and cursed;
Since erst we were hunted in rock and in clay,
And exiled to the terrible regions of day:
O that era, no time and no sorrows can blot,
When hunted by Reno, and found by La Motte:
O then what a series of griefs was begun,
What minerals plundered, what metals undone!
We were picked, and were hammered, bruised, injured, and broke,
And jostled in buckets, and smothered in smoke;
We were carried, like culprits, along in a cart,
And plunged in a furnace, and tortured with art:
So heedlessly handled, so rough, so severe,
Our injuries multiplied, year after year,
Till our woes and our insults all measure excel,

And we feel all the torments of roasting in hell.
And what is distressing beyond all our woes,
Our tears have turned gems in the chests of our foes;
Our blood and our groans have procured them delight,
And decked them with riches that dazzle the sight.
One only solace we have found for our woes,
'Tis the bullets we've sent to the hearts of our foes.
And yet all we feel in so high a degree,
O, king of the metals, is suffered for thee?
Go therefore on earth, men are panting for pelf,
Relieve our distress, and discover thyself."

He longer had spoken, but silver-faced Tin,
With air consequential, abruptly came in:
And, quoth he, "Out of pebbles and aggregate sand,
I am come from the depths to obey thy command;
But the place of my dwelling, my lonesome repose,
No name yet designates, no mortal yet knows;
'This a wilderness all; from the savage and deer,
No mischief I dread, and no sorrow I fear:
For they know not my usefulness, nature, or kind,
And they sweep o'er my home like a rattling wind.
This is all I may venture: a stranger to woe,
My heart is as light as a Chippewan doe;
And so sweetly I rest, so securely I lie,
That chemist and miner I both may defy."
Now Tin was a metal of Cornish descent,
Where the halcyon days of his boyhood were spent,
But his kin were so tortured, exhausted, distress'd,
He fled for relief to the woods of the west;
Where, although in retirement, remote, and unseen,
He often would boast of European kin;
Of friends he had left on the Gallic confines,
Or hid in the rocks of Bohemian mines;
Of German connexions, and boast that his name
Gave Devon her opulence, Cornwall her fame:
He would even advert to more elderly kin,
For Asia too, is a country of Tin:

But the thought of Siam, or of Banka ne'er rose,
Unmixed with a curse for his Belgian foes.
And while thus he descanted of ancestry free,
(Like brainless pretenders of mortal degree,)
Forgot that his friends were most bitterly poor,
Had endured many griefs, and had more to endure;
That their mines were expensive, exhausted, and old,
And worked at the price of the product when sold.
However, when thoughts so unpleasant oppress'd,
He brightened to think of his friends in the west:
How they all lay concealed from their enemies' sight,
Unburned by the miner, uncursed by the light;
And of all their rich ores in American ground,
In Chili alone had a morsel been found.

The next who addressed the imperial throne,
Now heaved a deep sigh, and now uttered a groan:
His rusty appearance, and sable attire,
Bespoke him afflicted by furnace and fire:
He seemed like some flinty, degenerate ore,
So dull was his visage, so earthy and poor;
And each bosom with manly compassion was shook,
When Iron thus pensive and feelingly spoke:
"If e'er sorrow wasted, or misery bent,
If pain e'er distracted, despair ever rent;
Or if injury wounded, or feeling oppress'd,
They now throb, they now rage, they now burn at my breast.
O my woes are unnumbered, and all of my race
Are plunged in despair, and o'erwhelmed in disgrace!
In vain we from country to country may roam,
No spot on the earth will afford us a home:
We are hunted on mountain, discovered in dale,
Nor will rock, nor will thicket, nor streamlet, avail:
In vain the earth hides us, in vain we may groan,
They find us in rocks, and extract us from stone:
All men are our foes, and unceasingly strive,
To catch us, and bruise us, and burn us alive;
And such is our number, and such are our fates,

We are found in all countries, oppressed in all states;
No rock but affords us, no soils but disclose,
Our place of concealment, our beds of repose;
And such is our rustic and simple disguise,
Every clown may detect, every zany descries.
Thus sought, and thus plighted, in misery high,
We hope not, we cannot—we droop, and we die;
For our very entrails they are gnawed and picked out,
And who lives without bowels is sturdy—no doubt."
Here, catching new spirit, he brightened his tone,
Paused, banished his sighs, and thus manly went on:
"Yet to all our distresses, for every woe,
No stop can we put, and no cure do we know;
For although, like my friend, the unfortunate Lead,
For your majesty thus we have suffered and bled;
Still my case is more cruel, my fate more severe,
And I still should be sought should you even appear.
For, though Gold is the object our enemies crave,
Iron too is of value, on land or on wave:
And though you in a gentleman's pocket may glow,
I only can furnish the farmer his plough."

If further of Iron, or its uses ye seek,
Bid Husbandry answer, let Chemistry speak;
No art but on this it is forced to depend,
For aid and assistance, a patron or friend;
Without it no trade could exist or progress,
And mechanics would fall on the tomb of distress.
Go call Navigation its use to support,
And Pharmacy summon, Astronomy court;
Metallurgy also, and Surgery call,
To join in the praise of this patron of all;
Let music and painting acknowledge its aids,
For sweetness of sounds, and for beauty of shades:
In fine, through all nature, all life, and all art,
See this favourite agent mix, enter, impart,
It fattens our soils, it impregnates our floods,
Tints the flowers of our gardens, the leaves of our woods,

We eat it in food, and we wear it in dress,
Our constant companion in health or distress.
It gives the rich hue to the gem of the mine,
And glows in the features of beauty divine:
The patron of arts, the philosopher's theme,
And favourite agent of wisdom supreme.

He scarcely had ceased, when with visage of ink,
A stranger approaching announced himself Zinc.
He was coldly received, till Galena, his friend,
Addressing the monarch, assured him 'twas Blende;
And he would not have ventured on taking the floor,
Unacquainted with Blende, or his use as an ore;
And the reason he had not metallic attire,
He ne'er had been tortured by furnace of fire.
Thus kindly excusing, without any fuss,
All ended, when Blende, with some modesty, thus:
"My home is Missouri, on Merrimack's shore
My relatives slumber, a numerous ore:
Mine Reno can witness, Potosi declare,
The wealth I possess, and the fame that I share:
But does any one hear me who doubting opines?
My proofs are at hand, I appeal to the mines;
But I still am a stranger to pain or distress,
My sorrows are little, my injuries less:
No pick-axe or hammer has battered my bones,
And I peacefully rest with my neighbouring stones:
For as few or my uses or properties scan,
I lie untormented by meddling man;
And whatever this august assembly decree,
But little affects or my kindred or me."

Now rosy-faced Copper, a metal of fame,
The wrongs of his country arose to proclaim.
His ancient descent we to periods trace,
Remote as the arts of the civilized race;
E'en the primitive ages his ores would amass,
And Tubal-Cain, he was a worker in brass.

To ages less distant he furnished employ,
Renowned throughout Egypt, Assyria, Troy.
So nobly descended, no wonder we trace
Some lines of ambition and fire in his face:
He talks of his ancestry, famous and high,
And proudly on new metals glances his eye,
As if crude, or of some alchemistic degree,
And doubting their honour, if smelted *per se.*

Such then were his claims, who succeeding address'd
The king of the metals, enthroned in the west:
"I rise with emotion my woes to reveal,
And boldly to speak what so strongly I feel;
Unprepared as I am, and all troubled within,
I hope I may still be of use to my kin:
And I trust—" (here he used some pathetic expression,
Exordium-like, or a kind of digression,
A rapture of feeling, a burst of the heart,
Peradventure a stroke of the congressman's art,
Which the muse who reported, and not being near,
Now fails to remember, as then to o'erhear.)
"But if any indulgence can justly accrue,
For services rendered or uses in view;
If aught can arise from chivalric degree,
It must now, potent monarch, be due unto me!
Supreme is my power, supreme my design,
I glow in the palace as well as the mine;
I serve in all places to show or excell,
I shine on the steeple, and ring in the bell,
I frown in the statue, in bronze, or in brass,
And thunder in cannon, and glitter in glass!
The seaman adores me, his needle and ship,
I both must encompass, adorn, and equip;
And the navy without me, our strength on the deep,
No foe could encounter, no glory could reap!
The painter without me would die of the spleen,
Deprived of his favourite beautiful green:
And wrought into wares as incongruous pile,

I cause merchants to flourish, and ladies to smile;
Whence a quadruple charm we in Copper can see,
Making wealth, beauty, valour, and fashion agree.
But I groan with distresses, I ache with despair,
And my kindred they die with the weight of their care.
Yet it is not from furnace or fire that they flow,
The miner's oak bucket, or ore-dresser's blow:
Ah, no! these create nor distress nor alarm,
For our virgin appearance secures us from harm.
Our home is a region all distant and drear,
Where the tempest is howling one half of the year;
Where the rock towers high, and the waters divide,
And Superior lashes the shore at our side.
Here, lone and neglected, my family groans,
Confined by the pressure of ponderous stones,
That are squeezing their bowels, and crushing their bones.
And so massy they are, and so heavy they lie,
That we grieve, and we tremble, we pant, and we die.
O, king of the metals, now hear our request!
Remove, we beseech you, the rocks from our breast;
Allow us the sun, and the air, and the light,
However exposed to our enemies sight;
For already oppressed with so weighty a curse,
A change may be better, but cannot be worse."
Who slowly now entered the parliament cave,
Looked sooty, and dark, unmetallic, and grave:
He bowed, but no one would his interest promote,
For Manganese n'er was a metal of note.
Though known to antiquity, hard was his case,
Called *oxyd,* and *metalloid, brittle,* and *base;*
And, although in the arts he was useful indeed,
Yet suffered for ages to languish and bleed—
Unclassed as a metal, unhonoured in books:
Till chemists began to examine his looks;
For though found as an oxyde, an earth-coloured ore,
They were pleased with his weight, and the texture he bore,
They studied his nature by acid and heat,
Then proved him a metal beyond a deceit;

Showed what were his uses, and dwelt on his part,
In the potter's and bleacher's and glassmaker's art.
Thus rescued from darkness they brightened his name,
And established for ever his title to fame.
When the monarch first summoned his metalline corps,
And convoked to the cave all his subjugate ores.
Black Manganese slumbered all peaceful in clay,
On Merrimack, hid from mankind and the day,
Whence rising he sought the congressional cave,
And entered all sooty, unpolished, and grave.
He bowed all respectful, then silently sat,
Now biting his fingers, now twirling his hat,
But spoke not, he wished, but had nothing to say,
And sat down to hear others debate, and obey.
A murmur without now announced the approach,
All hot, of a member who came in a coach,
And all eyes were directed to see and to know
What prince had arrived with such tumult and show:
But they shrunk with amazement, when bending in weeds,
A weeping, pale form, to the council proceeds.
So solemn, it seemed like a prodigal, rent
For estates he had squandered, or money mis-spent;
And many bethought some untoward design,
(Some mortal of Pluto in search, or a mine.)
Had news of their meeting, and came in disguise,
To seek and secure the auriferous prize:
That they all should be crowded with papers and dust,
In a miser's damp closet to slumber and rust:
Or proffer'd, as prospects should brighten or fail,
To keep rogues from the gallows, or thieves from the jail;
No eye but what sparkled, no heart but what beat,
And some thought of battle, and some of retreat;
Yet no murmur escaped, e'en the monarch of mines,
Nor thought of migrations, nor spoke of designs:
A silence ensued like the sleep of the dead,
So great was their panic, confusion, and dread.
But while thus they reflected in reverie high,
The stranger his veil threw all pensively by;

And they saw with delight a device on his breast,
Where silver commissioned the mystical guest:
'Twas the Genius of Paper, of bank-paper trash,
A substitute sent, both for honour and cash.
"You will pardon, (the genious desponding and weak,)
You will pardon my sorrows, I cannot yet speak:
I am weeping for woes which I cannot endure,
For evils I caused, but I never can cure.
I am pining for all that a nation can claim,
For honour, for character, credit, and fame:
And thus plunged in despair, and all buried in tears,
I have sighed for long months, I have wept for long years;
But all fruitless, my malady daily grows worse,
And the heavier my sorrows, the lighter my purse.
I first was suspected, it fretted me sad,
This grew to refusal, conviction, and bad;
And I daily sink deeper and deeper in woe,
And my friends are all broke, and to ruin we go.
I once was supported by silver—ah, me!
How fatal the friendship, we could not agree?
For as I grew in credit, he flew to retreats,
And slumbered in vaults, while I flaunted in streets;
And as I daily rose, so he daily declin'd,
Till a dollar in metal we scarcely could find.
So great my renown, it sunk deep on his heart,
And for once he determined the land to depart:
So he crept off in parcels, a dollar has legs,
And they waddled away both in boxes and kegs,
Till our banks they were empty, my kindred alone,
Now rule in oak drawers, and coffers of stone;
While he to those countries has taken a cruize,
Where paper's applied to a different use.
When therefore your majesty, vexed and in heat,
Bid all your dependents in Congress to meet,
There was only one dollar in silver, lone guest,
In all the dark vaults of the wide-spreading west;
Even that being funded, could not travel out,
Though he sighed and implored, the Cashier was a lout!

So he begged I would"—(here in a clamorous roar,
Echoed, "counterfeit—paper-rag—swindler, no more;")
And the king all enraged seized the genius with might,
And hurled him amain to the regions of night.

From so sad an affright, such tumultuous heats,
The members had scarcely arrived at their seats,
When a delegate reining a satin-white steed,
Alighting, announced himself Silver indeed,
He was plainly attired, and without any fuss,
Accosted the monarch full wittily thus:—
"My favours to win, and to find my retreat,
While mortals toil, jockey, drudge, murder, and cheat,
While merchants are broken, and lawyers are bent,
To gain my acquaintance—at twenty per cent.
For me, while the miser at midnight may groan,
And the creditor's turning his heart into stone,
While dullness through me, is for talents caress'd,
And merit without me, is merit unbless'd;
While for me, female beauty is worshipped by man,
And friendships are proffered, and hatreds began,
For me, while inventions and fashions are made,
And honour is sullied, and virtue betrayed;
Sure in such an assembly of metal as this,
I may safely all fears of detection dismiss;
And regardless of danger, unmindful of woes,
Describe the retreats where my kindred repose:
On Tennessee's borders they slumber in lime;
On Arkansaw known from the earliest time;
On Red River strewed by Almighty fiat.
And dispersed on the shores of the pleasant La Platte.
The Sabine, the Trinity, Teché, and Del Norde,
Glide smooth along banks which my treasures afford;
And my blood many a vein, nook, and cavity fills,
In Mexico's mountains, and quartz-covered hills.
For these I determine, for these I appear,
Their safety my trust, and their dangers my fear:
But I plead not for parleys, men cannot grow worse,

And I fear less their tortures than they do my curse."
Now members arrived in a body so dense,
A throng so tumultuous, motley, immense,
And so rapid they spoke, with such fury of word,
That the muse was unable to hear or record;
And so ill could she list to an orator's rave,
She determined to quit the congressional cave;
Yet before her departure recognised a few,
Whose forms were familiar, whose visage she knew.
There was Bismuth from Kanzas, and Scheele from the Plein;
And Nickel from Yazoo; and Prarie Du Chein;
Platina from Mora; from Erie Uran;
From Yellowstone Arsenic; Chrome, from Itan;
With Cobalt, and Mercury, high from the Stony;
Columbian, Cerium, gray Antimony,
All jumbled together in contact so hot,
'Twere hard to decide or who spoke or who not!
They bawled, and they ranted, they begged, and they press'd,
Now flush'd with delight, now with sorrow depress'd,
And such heats were begat among metals and stones,
That the cave filled with sulphur, and bellowed with groans;
And the earth, as if grasped by omnipotent might,
Quaked dreadful, and shook with the throes of affright;
Deep northwardly rolled the electrical jar,
Creating amazement, destruction, and war;
The rivers they boiled like a pot over coals,
And mortals fell prostrate and prayed for their souls:
Every rock on our borders cracked, quivered, and shrunk,
And Nackitosh tumbled, and New Madrid sunk.

Now the Monarch of Metals perceiving it vain,
Or the heats to allay, or the peace to regain,
Exerted a power to royalty dear,
And prorogued the convention to meet in a year;
But afterwards learning how mortals distress'd
Were shook with affright, and were leaving the west;
Exulted: he saw from an accident flow,
What planning and fighting might never bestow;

That the progress of empire was partly allayed;
That emigrants flagged, and plantations decayed;
And they now might repose without thinking with woe,
On the crucible, hammer, pick, bucket, and hoe;
That a spirit was dampened, which driving amain,
Forboded such grief to his golden domain;
And he fancied the dread would a season arrest,
The fame, population, and growth of the west.
When, therefore, the monarch maturely surveyed
The woeful effects which a quarrel had made,
All stately he rose, and proclaimed the behest,
Dissolving the sittings, and all was at rest.

So great was the tumult, confusion, and groans,
Such horrors arose from the clashing of stones.

Appendix: Schoolcraft's Itinerary and Modern Reference Maps

Readers who wish to visit particular sites or trace Schoolcraft's route in more detail should refer to the reference maps listed below. The list of maps includes 1:24,000 and 1:250,000 topographical quadrangles and county highway maps. The number in the parentheses by each topographic quadrangle refers to the order in which the map should be used in traveling along Schoolcraft's route from Potosi to the White River country and back. Some maps are used twice and both sequence numbers are included. The county highway maps are fully capitalized.

The column "Modern Environment and Landscape" includes commentary on the late-twentieth-century scene. Field notes were collected at various times over a period of several years, but mainly on trips taken between April 1993 and March 1995. The comments provide a basis for comparing the Ozark landscape of the 1990s with the scene Schoolcraft described.

DATE	ROUTE	MODERN ENVIRONMENT AND LANDSCAPE	REFERENCE MAPS
Thursday, November 5.	Potosi — first journal entry prior to departure on November 6.	Potosi (pop. 2,683), seat of Washington County, Missouri. Remains of mining era limited to names on street signs and brush-covered mine dumps in the surrounding area.	(1) Potosi 7.5' Quadrangle (MO) WASHINGTON COUNTY, MO
Friday, November 6.	Potosi to deserted Indian encampment on Bates Creek.	Scrubby oak-hickory forest dominant. The diameter of most trees is less than eighteen inches. Route parallel to Highway 8. Relief 150 to 230 feet.	(1) Potosi 7.5' Quadrangle (MO) WASHINGTON COUNTY, MO

DATE	ROUTE	MODERN ENVIRONMENT AND LANDSCAPE	REFERENCE MAPS
Saturday, November 7.	Bates Creek camp to hunter's cabin two miles east of the Fourche à Courtois (Courtois Creek).	Rough terrain with 100 to 200 feet local relief. The route cuts across the grain of the topography on the headwaters of the Fourche Renault and Lost Creek. Second-growth timber with patches of pasture on ridges. Schoolcraft reported that the uplands were mainly a savanna-like grassland in 1818.	(1) Potosi 7.5' Quadrangle (MO) (2) Shirley 7.5' Quadrangle (MO) (3) Courtois 7.5' Quadrangle (MO) WASHINGTON COUNTY, MO CRAWFORD COUNTY, MO
Sunday, November 8.	Hunter's cabin near Fourche à Courtois to encampment west of the Osage Fork of the Merrimack (Huzzah Creek).	Wooded upland. Some cleared pasture along Highway Y. Fenced fields in narrow alluvial valleys are now hay meadows and pastures. Little or no cultivated crops.Elevations 800 to 1100 feet. The Delaware and Shawnee encamped on Huzzah Creek had moved there from the eastern woodlands. The treaty with the Osage at Fort Osage in 1808 opened most of the Ozarks to settlement by whites and Native American tribes from the East. Some Delaware and Shawnee people had moved to the Ozarks as early as 1784 under the Spanish regime.	(3) Courtois 7.5' Quadrangle (MO) (4) Davisville 7.5' Quadrangle (MO) CRAWFORD COUNTY, MO
Monday, November 9.	Encampment near Huzzah Creek to prairie encampment near the Upper Meramec.	The route passed along the northern border of Indian Trail State Forest. Oak-hickory forest. Sparsely populated. Part-time livestock farming and forestry dominant. Canoe rentals and general stores near Courtois and Huzzah Creeks. Route passes near Davisville and Camel's Hump (elevation 1,343 feet).	(4) Davisville 7.5' Quadrangle (MO) (5) Cherryville 7.5' Quadrangle (MO) (6) Cook Station 7.5' Quadrangle (MO) CRAWFORD COUNTY, MO DENT COUNTY, MO

DATE	ROUTE	MODERN ENVIRONMENT AND LANDSCAPE	REFERENCE MAPS
Tuesday, November 10.	Prairie camp to encampment near a small lake in the upland prairie.	Open rolling upland with scattered woodlots. Fenced pastures and hay fields. Schoolcraft described the area as a "barren," a term he used often to describe the upland tracts. This is the southern part of the Salem Prairie, a karst region with numerous sinkholes. Many of them hold water.	(6) Cook Station 7.5' Quadrangle (MO) (7) Short Bend 7.5' Quadrangle (MO) (8) Doss 7.5' Quadrangle (MO) (9) Darien 7.5' Quadrangle (MO) DENT COUNTY, MO
Wednesday, November 11.	Traveled in a south-southwesterly direction, crossing a "Prairie of Little Lakes," to encampment on Cave Creek (Ashley Creek) one mile below Ashley Cave.	Fenced pastures on the Salem Prairie. A likely site for the "Prairie of Little Lakes" is the sinkhole tract north of Jadwin. Steep slopes encountered near the Upper Current River and Montauk State Park. Relief 200 to 300 feet, mostly sloping. Second-growth oak, hickory, and pine. Schoolcraft crossed the Current River between Montauk Spring and Cedar Grove. The river is part of the Ozark National Scenic Riverway.	(9) Darien 7.5' Quadrangle (MO) (10) Cedargrove 7.5' Quadrangle (MO) (11) Montauk 7.5' Quadrangle (MO) DENT COUNTY, MO
Thursday, November 12.	Explored caves on Cave Creek (Ashley Creek). Moved one mile up North Ashley Creek to Ashley Cave (SW 1/4, SW 1/4, Sec. 32, T32N, R7W).	Very steep slopes covered with oak, hickory, and shortleaf pine. The better stands of pine are on the uplands. County roads poor and stony, with mostly low-water bridges. Ashley Cave is on private property and can only be reached on foot or by heavy-duty vehicle. Schoolcraft overestimated the dimensions of the cave somewhat.	(11) Montauk 7.5' Quadrangle (MO) DENT COUNTY, MO

DATE	ROUTE	MODERN ENVIRONMENT AND LANDSCAPE	REFERENCE MAPS
Friday, November 13.	Explored Ashley Cave (Saltpeter Cave). Heavy rain.	The cave appears on the Montauk Quadrangle as Saltpeter Cave. Col. William Ashley abandoned mining at the cave in 1818 when an explosion occurred at his gunpowder works in Potosi. Ashley, a miner, surveyor, and real estate investor, served as Missouri's first lieutenant governor, 1820–24. He is best known as a leader in the development of the Rocky Mountain fur trade. The cave, heavily screened by timber and brush, is in the southeast bluff of North Ashley Creek.	(11) Montauk 7.5' Quadrangle (MO) DENT COUNTY, MO
Saturday, November 14.	Remained in the cave due to heavy rains.	North Ashley Creek has a narrow valley confined by very steep bluffs more than 200 feet high. Elevations 980 to 1280 feet.	(11) Montauk 7.5' Quadrangle (MO) DENT COUNTY, MO
Sunday, November 15.	From Ashley Cave to encampment on Bender Creek.	Steeply sloping land near North Ashley Creek. Thick stands of second-growth short-leaf pine. Very sparsely settled. Pasture and hay on ridges and valley bottomland support beef cattle agriculture. Large tracts of open pasture on the upland along Highway 137 south of Licking (pop. 1,328).	(11) Montauk 7.5' Quadrangle (MO) (12) Licking 7.5' Quadrangle (MO) (13) Raymondville 7.5' Quadrangle (MO) DENT COUNTY, MO TEXAS COUNTY, MO
Monday, November 16.	From Bender Creek southwest to encampment near West Piney Creek.	Rolling upland fescue pasture. Trees grow in small woodlots, creek valleys, and along fence rows. Route passed near Raymondville, seven miles east of Houston (pop. 2,118), the seat of Texas County. The Houston Prairie is a large karst upland with numerous sinkholes and small lakes. Larger houses and barns date from the turn-of-the-century general farming era.	(13) Raymondville 7.5' Quadrangle (MO) (14) Houston 7.5' Quadrangle (MO) (15) Bucyrus 7.5' Quadrangle (MO) TEXAS COUNTY, MO

DATE	ROUTE	MODERN ENVIRONMENT AND LANDSCAPE	REFERENCE MAPS
Tuesday, November 17.	From West Piney Creek south-southwest to encampment in a small valley.	Upland pasture with timber along the streams. The route passed near Cabool. Schoolcraft's limited knowledge of the region's geography, including the names of streams, is demonstrated by his speculation that they may have wandered into the headwaters of the Little Osage.	(15) Bucyrus 7.5' Quadrangle (MO) (16) Cabool NE 7.5' Quadrangle (MO) TEXAS COUNTY, MO
Wednesday, November 18.	Traveled southwest crossing the divide between the Missouri and Arkansas Rivers. Camped on a tributary of the North Fork of the White River (probably Panther Creek).	Upland pasture with timber along streams.	(16) Cabool NE 7.5' Quadrangle (MO) (17) Cabool NW 7.5' Quadrangle (MO) (18) Cabool SW 7.5' Quadrangle (MO)
Thursday, November 19.	South-southwest to encampment on a tributary of the Lime-Stone River (North Fork of the White River).	Transition from upland fescue pasture to forested hills in the headwaters of the North Fork.	(18) Cabool SW 7.5' Quadrangle (MO) (19) Nichols Knob 7.5' Quadrangle (MO) TEXAS COUNTY, MO
Friday, November 20.	South following the North Fork past Elkhorn (Topaz) Spring to encampment six miles above a large left-bank tributary, probably Indian Creek.	Very rugged terrain. Pastures limited to narrow ridgetops. Modest farmsteads on the uplands. Small frame houses. Few barns or other large outbuildings. Livestock farms produce mainly Hereford and Black Angus cattle. Sparsely populated.	(19) Nichols Knob 7.5' Quadrangle (MO) DOUGLAS COUNTY, MO

DATE	ROUTE	MODERN ENVIRONMENT AND LANDSCAPE	REFERENCE MAPS
Saturday, November 21.	South following the North Fork.	Continued wooded hills along the North Fork. The river bottom alluvial soils that grew thick stands of cane now support hay and pasture. No cultivated crops. The number of retirement and vacation homes along the river is increasing. Steep slopes and many vertical bluffs. Relief 150 to 250 feet.	(19) Nichols Knob 7.5' Quadrangle (MO) DOUGLAS COUNTY, MO
Sunday, November 22.	Southward on the western ridge avoiding the heavy cane in the North Fork bottoms. Camped in a cave (probably Potato Cave, NE 1/4, NW1/4, Sec. 32, T24N, R11W, Cureall NW 7.5' Quadrangle) in a bluff in Potato Cave Hollow, a tributary of the North Fork.	Mainly oak, hickory, and pine second-growth timber along the river breaks. Barbed-wire-fenced fescue pastures on the Dora upland. Numerous sinkholes and sinkhole ponds. The route passed near the small hamlet of Dora. Schoolcraft carved the date on a smooth rock in the cave, but no evidence of the carving remains.	(20) Dora 7.5' Quadrangle (MO) (21) Cureall 7.5' Quadrangle (MO) DOUGLAS COUNTY, MO OZARK COUNTY, MO
Monday, November 23.	Returned to the North Fork and followed it southward.	Sparsely populated by part-time farmers and a rural, non-farming population. Canoe rentals and general stores serve tourists and canoeists along the North Fork and Bryant Creek. Retirement and weekend homes are increasing in number along the river.	(21) Cureall 7.5' Quadrangle (MO) OZARK COUNTY, MO

DATE	ROUTE	MODERN ENVIRONMENT AND LANDSCAPE	REFERENCE MAPS
Tuesday, November 24.	Southward following the North Fork past Bryant Creek to deserted Indian camps near present-day Tecumseh, Missouri.	Very rugged terrain. Heavy cover of second-growth timber. Some pasture and hay on cleared ridges. Thin, poor soils. Tourist services at Dawt Mill. Slack water of Norfork Lake encountered just north of Tecumseh. Boat ramps and tourist and recreation services available at Tecumseh. The isolated "lost" hill at the mouth of Bryant Creek was formed by a cut-off meander of the North Fork. The cut off also accounts for the upstream flow of Bryant Creek at the streams' junction.	(21) Cureall NW 7.5' Quadrangle (MO) (22) Udall 7.5' Quadrangle (MO) OZARK COUNTY, MO
Wednesday, November 25.	Southward parallel to the North Fork to an abandoned cabin. Cane Creek, near its union with the North Fork, is a likely location for the cabin.	Rugged wooded hills. Some sections completely devoid of habitation.	(22) Udall 7.5' Quadrangle (MO) OZARK COUNTY, MO
Thursday, November 26.	Due to the large increase in size of the North Fork, the travelers were confused about whether or not they were on the North Fork or the White River itself. Schoolcraft crossed to the west side of the river and walked upstream in search of a large stream. Remained at the cabin on Cane Creek.	Steep forested slopes, narrow valleys, and ridges with little cleared land.	(22) Udall 7.5' Quadrangle (MO) OZARK COUNTY, MO
Friday, November 27.	South-southwest on the ridge parallel to the river. Camped in an Indian bark hut.	Sparsely populated wooded hill country. Lake-front homes increasing in number.	(23) Bakersfield 7.5' Quadrangle (MO) (24) Gamaliel 7.5' Quadrangle (AR) OZARK COUNTY, MO BAXTER COUNTY, AR

DATE	ROUTE	MODERN ENVIRONMENT AND LANDSCAPE	REFERENCE MAPS
Saturday, November 28.	Provisions depleted. Traveled south-southwest on the east ridge bordering the river. Camped on the river bank and had acorns for supper.	Sparsely populated wooded hill country. Scattered retirement and vacation homes near Norfork Lake.	(24) Gamaliel 7.5' Quadrangle (AR) BAXTER COUNTY, AR
Sunday, November 29.	Traveled south-southeast to a dry encampment in a deep ravine.	Sparsely populated hill country. Cedar glades common, some with bare rock exposed.	(24) Gamaliel 7.5' Quadrangle (AR) BAXTER COUNTY, AR
Monday, November 30.	Discovered a horsepath and followed it northeast. Encountered a hunter on horseback and accompanied him northeast to a cabin on Bennet's Bayou owned by a settler identified only as "Wells."	Wooded hills. Cedar glades on ridges. Very thin stony soils with some bare rock surfaces. Prickly pear cactus present in some cedar glades.	(24) Gamaliel 7.5' Quadrangle (AR) BAXTER COUNTY, AR OZARK COUNTY, MO
Tuesday, December 1.	Made moccasins and ground corn meal. Returned to the hunter's camp on the North Fork to pick up their equipment and horse.	Mainly second-growth oak timber, the diameter of most trees is less than eighteen inches.	(24) Gamaliel 7.5' Quadrangle (MO) OZARK COUNTY, MO
Wednesday, December 2.	Spent the day at the North Fork hunter's camp making moccasins and taking stock of their situation.	The site of the hunter's cabin is inundated by Norfork Lake, which has a normal pool elevation of 546 feet above mean sea level.	(24) Gamaliel 7.5' Quadrangle (MO) (25) Bakersfield 7.5' Quadrangle (MO) (26) Udall 7.5' Quadrangle (MO) OZARK COUNTY, MO
Thursday, December 3.	Spent the day at the North Fork hunter's camp preparing to continue the journey.	Settlement on the Cane Creek arm and nearby shores of Norfork Lake is sparse due to the limited number of access roads through the hilly terrain surrounding the lake.	(26) Udall 7.5' Quadrangle (MO) OZARK COUNTY, MO

DATE	ROUTE	MODERN ENVIRONMENT AND LANDSCAPE	REFERENCE MAPS
Friday, December 4.	Confined to camp by rain.	Norfork Lake, like most Ozark lakes, is bordered by steep forested slopes. Nearly vertical bluffs identify the eroded side of meander loops cut by the North Fork River.	(26) Udall 7.5' Quadrangle (MO) OZARK COUNTY, MO
Saturday, December 5.	Departed west in search of the settlement at Sugarloaf Prairie on the White River. Camped on a small tributary of the North Fork, most likely Lick Creek.	Rough, sparsely populated hill country. Cleared pasture limited to narrow ridges and to small patches of alluvial soil along streams flowing into Bull Shoals Lake.	(26) Udall 7.5' Quadrangle (MO) (27) Gainesville 7.5' Quadrangle (MO) OZARK COUNTY, MO
Sunday, December 6.	Traveled west-southwest and encamped on the Little North Fork of the White River.	Oak, hickory, and pine forest on steep slopes. Small clearings on some uplands. Schoolcraft's camp site is now flooded by the Little North Fork arm of Bull Shoals Lake.	(27) Gainesville 7.5' Quadrangle (MO) (28) Isabella 7.5' Quadrangle (MO) OZARK COUNTY, MO
Monday, December 7.	Traveled west six miles, then south to the cabin of Mr. M'Gary (probably James McGarrah) on the White River.	Mainly sloping land. Nearly vertical bluffs along the White River. Cedar glades on very thin stony soils. The unnamed bald knob north of M'Gary's cabin site is now wooded to the top. Holt Bald, four miles north-northwest, is also completely wooded.	(28) Isabella 7.5' Quadrangle (MO) (29) Theodosia 7.5' Quadrangle (MO) (30) Cotter NW 7.5' Quadrangle (AR) OZARK COUNTY, MO MARION COUNTY, AR
Tuesday, December 8.	Traveled north-northwest (upstream) on the east side of the White River sixteen miles.	The White River valley is now flooded by Bull Shoals Lake. Schoolcraft's ridgetop route is now mainly scrubby oak-hickory woodland interrupted by occasional cedar glades. Some broad uplands have been cleared for pasture.	(30) Cotter NW 7.5' Quadrangle (MO) (31) Theodosia 7.5' Quadrangle (MO) (32) Protem 7.5' Quadrangle (MO) (33) Peel 7.5' Quadrangle (AR) MARION COUNTY, AR

DATE	ROUTE	MODERN ENVIRONMENT AND LANDSCAPE	REFERENCE MAPS
Wednesday, December 9.	Continued upstream to Mr. Coker's cabin at Sugarloaf Prairie. This was probably Lem Coker, a settler from eastern Tennessee. According to *The White River Chronicles of S. C. Turnbo,* Lem, or "Buck," Coker settled on the lower end of Jake Nave Bend on the White River. He was the patriarch of the Boone County, Arkansas, Coker clan.	Sugarloaf Prairie lies between Lead Hill and Diamond City. Schoolcraft described Sugarloaf Knob (elevation 969 feet; NW 1/4, Sec. 33, T21N, R18W, Diamond City 7.5' Quadrangle) as a "bald" hill. Today it is forested to the top. Diamond City, formerly called Sugarloaf, is a lake resort community with a large marina and a U.S. Army Corps of Engineers Public Use Area. Diamond City was founded in the 1950s when Bull Shoals Lake was formed. The prairie is now fenced pasture land with scattered rural homes.	(33) Peel 7.5' Quadrangle (AR) (34) Diamond City 7.5' Quadrangle (AR) BOONE COUNTY, AR
Thursday, December 10.	Traveled eight miles northwest. Camped under a limestone shelf.	Rugged hilly terrain with numerous isolated knob hills. Steep bluffs border Bull Shoals Lake. Sparsely populated except near the lake where retirement and vacation home development contributes to population growth.	(34) Diamond City 7.5' Quadrangle (AR) (35) Protem SW 7.5' Quadrangle (MO) (36) Mincy 7.5' Quadrangle (MO) MARION COUNTY, AR
Friday, December 11.	Continued northwest eighteen miles to a cold camp after fording the White River.	Steep sloping wooded hills bordering Table Rock Lake. Boat ramps, marinas, and second homes are evidence of recent settlement and increasing population.	(36) Mincy 7.5' Quadrangle (MO) TANEY COUNTY, MO

DATE	ROUTE	MODERN ENVIRONMENT AND LANDSCAPE	REFERENCE MAPS
Saturday, December 12.	Continued along the river six miles to the last settlement on the White River, the cabins of William Holt and James Fisher, approximately one mile above the mouth of Beaver Creek. (Although Schoolcraft identifies the settlers only as "Holt" and "Fisher," Lankford provides their given names.) The cabins were built on an alluvial bottom along a meander loop in the White River. Two natural rock pyramids at the top of the steep bluff on the opposite riverbank cast their shadows across the bottomlands in the afternoon.	Although Cathedral Cave (NW 1/4, SE 1/4, SW 1/4, NE 1/4, NW 1/4, Sec. 2, T22N, R19W, Forsyth 7.5' Quadrangle) is only about three miles from the cabins above Beaver Creek, it fits Schoolcraft's description closely. A large boat rental and marina occupies the west bank of the Beaver Creek arm where it branches from Table Rock Lake. The site of the Holt and Fisher cabins appears to be cultivated and planted in crops (primarily grain sorghum) during low lake levels. The two natural pyramids at the crest of Johnson Bluff on the opposite shore are present, but are less prominent than Schoolcraft described them.	(37) Forsyth 7.5' Quadrangle (MO) TANEY COUNTY, MO
Sunday, December 13–Sunday, December 27.	Employed at the Beaver Creek settlement hewing planks and building cabins.	Several newer houses have been built on the bluff north of the old Beaver Creek cabin site. Bluffs bordering the lake are prime for second homes and retirement homes because of the advantages for a panoramic view.	(37) Forsyth 7.5' Quadrangle (MO) TANEY COUNTY, MO
Monday, December 28.	Traveled north toward the Pearson Creek lead mine guided by Holt and Fisher. Camped at the foot of Helphrey Hill (SE 1/4, Sec. 15, T24N, R19W, Garrison 7.5' Quadrangle) near Taneyville, Missouri.	Very rugged wooded hills in the Beaver and Swan creek basins. Helphrey Hill (elevation 1,210 feet), a prominent bald knob, is now wooded over. Swan and Bull Creeks are gravelly, shallow, and clear. Numerous abandoned farms tell of a heavier valley population in the past. Recent settlement is mainly confined to the ridges, especially on land bordering the Mark Twain National Forest.	(37) Forsyth 7.5' Quadrangle (MO) (38) Garrison 7.5' Quadrangle (MO) TANEY COUNTY, MO

DATE	ROUTE	MODERN ENVIRONMENT AND LANDSCAPE	REFERENCE MAPS
Tuesday, December 29.	Continued northwest to Swan Creek. Camped in the valley of Swan Creek southeast of Oldfield.	Slopes wooded. Cedar glades on the southern and western slopes. The abandoned roadbed of the Chadwick Branch of the St. Louis & San Francisco Railroad is visible at Oldfield. The railroad ceased operations during the 1930s after removal of the virgin pine and oak timber. Chadwick's vacant lots and relict building foundations, like those of dozens of former sawmill towns, tell the story of population decline following the removal of the virgin timber.	(38) Garrison 7.5' Quadrangle (MO) (39) Chadwick 7.5' Quadrangle (MO) CHRISTIAN COUNTY, MO
Wednesday, December 30.	Continued northwest passing near Oldfield and camped in Carter Hollow, a tributary of Finley Creek.	Rugged hills with 200 to 300 feet relief. Route passes through the Mark Twain National Forest.	(39) Chadwick 7.5' Quadrangle (MO) (40) Rogersville 7.5' Quadrangle (MO) CHRISTIAN COUNTY, MO
Thursday, December 31.	Continued north to Finley Creek and followed it east.	Upland fescue pastures with wooded hillsides. Suburban residences replacing farms. The growth of greater Springfield, Missouri, is causing rapid change from rural-farm to rural non-farm population.	(40) Rogersville 7.5' Quadrangle (MO) (41) Ozark 7.5' Quadrangle (MO) CHRISTIAN COUNTY, MO
Friday, January 1.	Traveled downstream along the Finley River stopping at Smallin Cave. Camped near the lead deposit on the James River at the mouth of Pearson Creek.	The surface of the rolling upland of the Springfield Plain bordering the Finley River is mainly fescue pasture. Suburban settlement is encroaching on dairy and livestock farms. Smallin Cave (briefly operated commercially, circa 1970, as Civil War Cave) is now a summer camp site for the Assemblies of God Church.	(41) Ozark 7.5' Quadrangle (MO) (42) Galloway 7.5' Quadrangle (MO) CHRISTIAN COUNTY, MO GREENE COUNTY, MO

DATE	ROUTE	MODERN ENVIRONMENT AND LANDSCAPE	REFERENCE MAPS
Saturday, January 2–Monday, January 4.	Encamped at the mouth of Pearson Creek examining the lead diggings and assessing the surroundings.	The encampment site is one-half mile east of Springfield's eastern boundary. The area is experiencing rapid buildup with new middle- and upper-range suburban dwellings. In 1921 the Rotary Club of Springfield placed a marker at Kerchner's Spring near Schoolcraft's riverside camp-site to commemorate his visit. Mining operations between 1870 and 1893 in the Pearson Creek Mining District produced $567,700 in lead and zinc ores. Sporadic mining continued into the 1930s until the ores were depleted.	(42) Galloway 7.5' Quadrangle (MO) GREENE COUNTY, MO
Tuesday, January 5.	Set out south toward the Beaver Creek cabins and camped on Upper Bull Creek.	The route south via the valleys of Bull Creek and Swan Creek passes through the rugged timber land in the Mark Twain National Forest. Valley roads are rough and winding and streams are crossed by low-water bridges.	(42) Galloway 7.5' Quadrangle (MO) (43) Ozark 7.5' Quadrangle (MO) (44) Chadwick 7.5' Quadrangle (MO) GREENE COUNTY, MO CHRISTIAN COUNTY, MO
Wednesday, January 6.	Continued south following Bull Creek crossing into Swan Creek valley before darkness.	Very sparsely settled hills covered with oak, hickory, and pine. Cedar glades are common. Suburban settlement increasing, especially on the northern borders of the Mark Twain National Forest. Subdivided land in parcels of ten to twenty acres is being sold for suburban homes and "farmettes."	(44) Chadwick 7.5' Quadrangle (MO) CHRISTIAN COUNTY, MO

DATE	ROUTE	MODERN ENVIRONMENT AND LANDSCAPE	REFERENCE MAPS
Thursday, January 7.	Continued south in a heavy snowstorm following Swan Creek past Helphrey Hill to the Beaver Creek cabins.	Helphrey Hill owes its landmark attribute more to its conspicuously isolated location than to remarkable elevation.	(45) Garrison 7.5' Quadrangle (MO) (46) Forsyth 7.5' Quadrangle (MO) TANEY COUNTY, MO
Friday, January 8.	Remained at the cabins near the mouth of Beaver Creek making preparations for the canoe trip down the White River to Poke Bayou (Batesville).	At the normal pool level of 654 feet elevation, the bottomland at the Beaver Creek cabins site is dry, but during flood pool it is inundated.	(46) Forsyth 7.5' Quadrangle (MO) TANEY COUNTY, MO
Saturday, January 9.	Set out down the White River traveling by canoe. Stayed at Mr. Yochem's cabin two miles above the mouth of Bear Creek. This was probably Solomon Yocum. According to Turnbo, Yocum later settled in Stone County, Missouri, where he was a principal figure in the distillation of whiskey and its illegal sale to immigrant Indians.	The White River valley is flooded by the waters of Bull Shoals Lake. Bluffs wooded, some upland cleared for pasture. Land subdivision and house construction is expanding near the lake.	(46) Forsyth 7.5' Quadrangle (MO) (47) Mincy 7.5' Quadrangle (MO) TANEY COUNTY, MO
Sunday, January 10.	Traveled from Yochem's cabin to Lem "Buck" Coker's cabin opposite Sugarloaf Prairie.	This section of the river is under Bull Shoals Lake. The settlement landscape is a mixture of older farm houses and newer-style houses reflecting increased numbers of retirees and other rural non-farm inhabitants.	(47) Mincy 7.5' Quadrangle (MO) (48) Omaha NE 7.5' Quadrangle (MO) (49) Diamond City 7.5' Quadrangle (AR) BOONE COUNTY, AR

DATE	ROUTE	MODERN ENVIRONMENT AND LANDSCAPE	REFERENCE MAPS
Monday, January 11.	Traveled forty miles on the river from Coker's cabin to M'Gary's cabin, situated on the right bank and facing the mouth of the Little North Fork River.	The river route is now under Bull Shoals Lake. The Little North Fork River valley forms a northern arm of the lake.	(49) Diamond City 7.5' Quadrangle (AR) (50) Peel 7.5' Quadrangle (AR) (51) Cotter NW 7.5' Quadrangle (AR) BOONE COUNTY, AR
Tuesday, January 12.	Encountered the Bull Shoals (rapids) twenty miles below M'Gary's and passed through with difficulties. Stopped at the cabin of August Friend below the shoals.	The landscape is much modified by the Bull Shoals Dam site, access roads, residential development, and tourist services. Cedar glades with barren rock surfaces are interspersed with second-growth timber on uplands. The lake resort communities of Bull Shoals and Lakeview are examples of several new towns built near the Ozarks' large lakes.	(51) Cotter NW 7.5' Quadrangle (AR) (52) Bull Shoals 7.5' Quadrangle (AR) (53) Cotter 7.5' Quadrangle (AR) MARION COUNTY, AR
Wednesday, January 13.	Examined Indian artifacts and mineral deposits near Friend's cabin, then traveled downstream to J. Yochem's cabin. This was probably Jacob Yocum.	The terrain bordering the lake is steeply sloping and heavily forested with oak-hickory timber and occasional stands of pine. Bold bluffs mark former erosion work of the White River.	(53) Cotter 7.5' Quadrangle (AR) MARION COUNTY, AR
Thursday, January 14.	Loaned canoe to Jacob Yochem to transport meat to a trader at the mouth of the North Fork. Schoolcraft and Pettibone traveled overland to Matney's cabin opposite the mouth of the "Great North Fork." This was probably William Matney, whose cabin was on the right bank of the White River opposite the cabins of the Adams and Wolf families.	The hamlet of Norfork, Arkansas, occupies a rock shelf on Highway 5 just below the mouth of the North Fork of the White River. The Wolf House, a rare two-story, four-pen log house with a dog-trot passage, is said to have been erected circa 1826 by Jacob Wolf, a blacksmith and trader. It replaced a smaller cabin built by Wolf when he occupied the site in 1809. The view of the junction of the two rivers from the Wolf House is impressive.	(53) Cotter 7.5' Quadrangle (AR) (54) Mountain Home West 7.5' Quadrangle (AR) (55) Buffalo City 7.5' Quadrangle (AR) (56) Norfork 7.5' Quadrangle (AR) BAXTER COUNTY, AR

DATE	ROUTE	MODERN ENVIRONMENT AND LANDSCAPE	REFERENCE MAPS
Friday, January 15.	Delayed by the late arrival of the canoe. Examined surrounding countryside. Schoolcraft described "a fragment of red granite" as one of the minerals he collected. This rock specimen is not native to either the White or North Fork river basins. Schoolcraft was a skilled practical mineralogist, but may have been mistaken in his identification of the specimen.	The landscape at the mouth of the North Fork is especially scenic. It is comprised of deciduous hardwoods and shortleaf pine with patches of rocky cedar glades. Local relief is 250 to 300 feet with very steep slopes and nearly vertical bluffs bordering the rivers. At Red Bluff the river has exposed nearly 400 feet of sedimentary rock strata where it gouges into Matney's Knob. Local relief at the knob is nearly 900 feet.	(56) Norfork 7.5' Quadrangle (AR) BAXTER COUNTY, AR
Saturday, January 16.	After unloading their canoe and witnessing a night of heavy drinking by the hunters, Schoolcraft and Pettibone continued down river past Calico Rock and stopped fourteen miles below the bluff at Jeffrey's cabin. This was probably Jehoida Jeffery, a Virginian of English parentage.	The town of Calico Rock (pop. 1,200) is situated on the multicolored half-mile-long bluff rising vertically from the White River. At the foot of Calico Bluff, as it is now called, are lodging and boat rentals for trout anglers. The view of Calico Bluff from Highway 5 south of the town is impressive.	(56) Norfork 7.5' Quadrangle (AR) (57) Norfork Dam South 7.5' Quadrangle (AR) (58) Calico Rock 7.5' Quadrangle (AR) (59) Boswell 7.5' Quadrangle (AR) BAXTER COUNTY, AR STONE COUNTY, AR
Sunday, January 17.	Continued downstream thirty-five miles to the Widow Lafferty's settlement on the west bank. John Lafferty settled on the right bank of the White River in 1810, but had to move to the opposite bank near the mouth of Lafferty Creek when the land between the White and Arkansas Rivers was granted to the Cherokees in 1818.	Nearly vertical river bluffs with relief 250–350 feet. Broader alluvial river bottoms, some large enough to be named (e.g., Jones Bottom, Smith Island). Some cultivated crops. Hillsides wooded with small clearings on ridges. Some uplands, or "flats," are large enough to be named.	(60) Sylamore 7.5' Quadrangle (AR) (61) Guion 7.5' Quadrangle (AR) (62) Mount Pleasant 7.5' Quadrangle (AR) (63) Bethesda 7.5' Quadrangle (AR) STONE COUNTY, AR

DATE	ROUTE	MODERN ENVIRONMENT AND LANDSCAPE	REFERENCE MAPS
Monday, January 18.	Continued downstream past the cabin of Mr. Jones, then past Hardin's Ferry and Morrison's Ferry to Poke Bayou (Batesville). On leaving Lafferty's, the adventurers passed several cabins, including those of the Hess and O'Neal families, which had been there since 1814. He mentioned the Jones family (probably Stephen Jones) and Hardin's Ferry, then operated by Joab Hardin. He failed to mention George Ruddell, who operated a mill on Dry Creek just above Poke Bayou. Hurrying to set out for Potosi, Schoolcraft recorded only brief mention of a few settlers and a hasty description of Poke Bayou, the only town he had seen on the river.	Attractive river and wooded-hill-country scenery. Broader valleys but substantial relief. Round Mountain (Sec. 22, T13N, R8W; elevation 1,150 feet) rises 800 feet above the river. Batesville (pop. 9,187), the seat of Independence County, Arkansas, is the largest town in the southeastern Ozarks. It is built on the Ozark Escarpment, or bluff, where the White River exits the Ozarks. Elevations 250 to 530 feet. Batesville is sharing in the rapid growth of northern Arkansas (which appears to be tied to the shift of industries to the South), the rapid growth of the service sector of the economy, and the increase of population in areas that have amenities.	(63) Bethesda 7.5' Quadrangle (AR) (64) Concord 7.5' Quadrangle (AR) (65) Batesville 7.5' Quadrangle (AR) INDEPENDENCE COUNTY, AR
Tuesday, January 19.	Departed Poke Bayou following the Southwest Trail, or Arkansas Road (later called the Military Road and the Texas Trail). Stopped at a cabin after traveling eighteen miles. Schoolcraft sprained his ankle.	The Southwest Trail followed the rolling hills along the Ozark Escarpment parallel to U.S. 67 and Arkansas 115. The trail followed the upland to avoid the trackless swamps in the Mississippi Alluvial Plain. Elevations 260 to 510 feet. Mixed woodland, pasture, and cropland.	(65) Batesville 7.5' Quadrangle (AR) (66) Sulphur Rock 7.5' Quadrangle (AR) (67) Grange 7.5' Quadrangle (AR) INDEPENDENCE COUNTY, AR
Wednesday, January 20.	Continued northeast to the Strawberry River with Schoolcraft riding a traveler's horse.	Schoolcraft crossed the "south fork" of Strawberry River at a small hamlet. This was probably Calamine, Arkansas, on South Big Creek. Streams issuing from the Ozarks in this section have broad flood plains with hills rising only 100 to 150 feet. Elevations above mean sea level range between 250 and 350 feet on the uplands.	(67) Grange 7.5' Quadrangle (AR) (68) Poughkeepsie 7.5' Quadrangle (AR) (69) Smithville 7.5' Quadrangle (AR) LAWRENCE COUNTY, AR

DATE	ROUTE	MODERN ENVIRONMENT AND LANDSCAPE	REFERENCE MAPS
Thursday, January 21.	Pettibone traveled on alone. Schoolcraft remained at the farmhouse to rest his ankle. (Pettibone, in a short report on the trip written many years later, maintained that the two men did not separate until near Ste. Genevieve, Missouri.)	Schoolcraft spent the day at the farmhouse resting his sprained ankle.	(69) Smithville 7.5' Quadrangle (AR) LAWRENCE COUNTY, AR
Friday, January 22.	Schoolcraft continued northeast following the Southwest Trail stopping at Dogwood Spring.	Dogwood Spring is in the source area for Dogwood Branch of East Cooper Creek near the divide between the Strawberry and Spring Rivers. Rolling oak-covered hills with pasture on more level areas.	(69) Smithville 7.5' Quadrangle (AR) (70) Ravenden 7.5' Quadrangle (AR) LAWRENCE COUNTY, AR
Saturday, January 23.	Continued northeast to Spring River near present-day Imboden.	Wooded hills give way to fields of soybeans and grain sorghum on bottomlands near Imboden. Slopes in second-growth oak.	(70) Ravenden 7.5' Quadrangle (AR) (71) Imboden 7.5' Quadrangle (AR) LAWRENCE COUNTY, AR
Sunday, January 24.	Crossed Spring River in a canoe then continued on. Crossed the Eleven Point River and reached the Fourche à Thomas (Fourche River) by nightfall.	The northeasterly route cuts across the grain of topography shaped by streams exiting the Ozarks from the northwest. Wooded uplands alternate with cultivated bottomlands.	(71) Imboden 7.5' Quadrangle (AR) (72) Noland 7.5' Quadrangle (AR) (73) Ravenden Spring SE 7.5' Quadrangle (AR) (74) Pocahontas 7.5' Quadrangle (AR) LAWRENCE COUNTY, AR

DATE	ROUTE	MODERN ENVIRONMENT AND LANDSCAPE	REFERENCE MAPS
Monday, January 25.	Crossed the Fourche à Thomas, then continued northeast crossing the Current River at Hicks' Ferry (Current View). Stopped at a cabin six miles beyond the Current River.	Broad alluvial valleys extend along the major streams exiting from the Ozarks. Hills are covered with second-growth oak-hickory forest. Relief 100 to 150 feet.	(74) Pocahontas 7.5' Quadrangle (AR) (75) Maynard 7.5' Quadrangle (AR-MO) (76) Supply 7.5' Quadrangle (AR-MO) (77) Doniphan South 7.5' Quadrangle (MO) (78) Oxly 7.5' Quadrangle (MO) LAWRENCE COUNTY, AR RIPLEY COUNTY, MO
Tuesday, January 26.	Traveled northeast following the Southwest Trail and camped two miles beyond the Little Black River.	The route again penetrates into the rugged hill country of the southeastern Ozarks. The limestone plateau is much dissected, with most of the area in steep slopes. Heavily wooded with oak, hickory, and scattered stands of pine.	(78) Oxly 7.5' Quadrangle (MO) (79) Flatwoods 7.5' Quadrangle (MO) RIPLEY COUNTY, MO
Wednesday, January 27.	Continued on to the Black River and crossed the river in a canoe. Found lodging at a house a mile beyond the river.	The Southwest Trail crossed the Black River near Hendrickson in northern Butler County, Missouri. The mile-wide flood plain is bounded by wooded hills. Uplands hilly and forested. The fertile bottomland produces the chief crops (corn, wheat, grain sorghum, and soybeans) grown in the adjacent Mississippi alluvial basin.	(80) Hogan Hollow 7.5' Quadrangle (MO) (81) Williamsville 7.5' Quadrangle (MO) RIPLEY COUNTY, MO BUTLER COUNTY, MO WAYNE COUNTY, MO

DATE	ROUTE	MODERN ENVIRONMENT AND LANDSCAPE	REFERENCE MAPS
Thursday, January 28.	Traveled north on the Southwest Trail. Crossed the St. Francis River at Bettis' Ferry (site of old Greenville before it was inundated by Lake Wappapello).	Hilly terrain covered with oak, hickory, and scattered stands of pine. General elevations 400 to 650 feet. After the construction of Wappapello Dam, twenty miles southeast on the St. Francis River, Greenville (pop. 393) spread to the adjacent uplands above the flooded valley. Greenville's only industry is a small pallet company that employs about a dozen workers.	(81) Williamsville 7.5' Quadrangle (MO) (82) Piedmont 7.5' Quadrangle (MO) (83) Greenville SW 7.5' Quadrangle (MO) (84) Greenville 7.5' Quadrangle (MO) WAYNE COUNTY, MO
Friday, January 29.	Continued north toward St. Michael's (Fredericktown) in a driving rain. Stopped at a cabin seven miles beyond Bettis' Ferry.	Relief increases as the route penetrates the St. Francois Mountains. Most of the prominent mountains are named. Little level land. Slopes are heavily forested with second-growth timber. Few areas of pasture or cultivated land.	(84) Greenville 7.5' Quadrangle (MO) (85) Coldwater 7.5' Quadrangle (MO) WAYNE COUNTY, MO MADISON COUNTY, MO
Saturday, January 30.	Continued north, turning off on the road to Belleview, and lodged near the St. Francis River.	Heavily wooded granite and rhyolite ridges and knobs with narrow intervening valleys.	(85) Coldwater 7.5' Quadrangle (MO) (86) Rock Pile Mountain 7.5' Quadrangle (MO) (87) Rhodes Mountain 7.5' Quadrangle (MO) MADISON COUNTY, MO

DATE	ROUTE	MODERN ENVIRONMENT AND LANDSCAPE	REFERENCE MAPS
Sunday, January 31.	Attempted to cross the St. Francis, but the rain-swollen river was too high. Continued north along the Little St. Francis River to a cabin four miles downstream from St. Michael's.	Modern Fredericktown (pop. 3,950) lies in a basin of sedimentary rock. The area's fertile soils formerly supported crops of corn and small grains. Today the rolling plain is mainly in pasture and very little land is cultivated. Forested "hard rock" igneous knobs and ridges protruding through the sedimentary rocks give the basin an appealing landscape. Fredericktown's focus is the public square, which serves both as the commercial core and the site of the striking red-brick Madison County Courthouse.	(87) Rhodes Mountain 7.5' Quadrangle (MO) MADISON COUNTY, MO
Monday, February 1.	Returned to the Little St. Francis River to observe and study the Narrows, one of many "shut-ins," or river gorges, in the St. Francois Mountains. The journal is unclear at this point. There are numerous "shut-ins" in the vicinity and another interpretation is that the Narrows is the Silvermine Shut-in on the St. Francis River. However, Schoolcraft notes that the Narrows is close by St. Michael's, which would place it on the Little St. Francis River. This corresponds to Schoolcraft's description of traveling up the "northeast branch" of the St. Francis River. The Narrows of the Little St. Francis River (Sec. 14, T33N, R6E, Fredericktown 7.5' Quadrangle) is about two miles southwest of Fredericktown.	The Narrows is formed where the river cuts between Buckner Mountain (elevation 946 feet) and Mount Devon (elevation 1,119 feet), about two miles southwest of Fredericktown. The boulder-choked river channel is confined to a narrow gorge cut in granite and rhyolite.	(87) Rhodes Mountain 7.5' Quadrangle (MO) (88) Fredericktown 7.5' Quadrangle (MO) MADISON COUNTY, MO

DATE	ROUTE	MODERN ENVIRONMENT AND LANDSCAPE	REFERENCE MAPS
Tuesday, February 2.	Failed in an attempt to cross the Little St. Francis River at the upper ford. Continued through St. Michael's (Fredericktown) and Mine La Motte to Cook's settlement.	The basin floor is mainly open pastures with timber growing along streams and on the steep slopes of mountains.	(88) Fredericktown 7.5' Quadrangle (MO) (89) Knob Lick 7.5' Quadrangle (MO) MADISON COUNTY, MO
Wednesday, February 3.	Continued north through Murphy's settlement (Farmington) to Hale's settlement (Desloge) on Big River.	Farmington (pop. 11,598) is the seat of St. Francois County and the principal town in the Farmington basin. It is a trade and service center with several manufacturing plants producing clothing, shoes, modular houses, structural steel, and automobile parts. When first established in 1798, the settlement was named Murphy's to honor one of the first settlers. Old mine dumps and tailings piles are visible from Highway OO at Mine La Motte.	(89) Knob Lick 7.5' Quadrangle (MO) (90) Farmington 7.5' Quadrangle (MO) (91) Flat River 7.5' Quadrangle (MO) ST. FRANCOIS COUNTY, MO
Thursday, February 4.	Followed the road directly to Potosi arriving at 3:00 PM "after an absence of ninety days, and having travelled more than nine hundred miles." Schoolcraft's route followed that of U.S. Highway 67 and Missouri Highway 8 to Potosi.	Second-growth oak-hickory forest. Hilly terrain with elevations between 950 and 1,100 feet. Brush-covered mine dumps are evidence of long-abandoned mines.	(91) Flat River 7.5' Quadrangle (MO) (92) Irondale 7.5' Quadrangle (MO) (93) Mineral Point 7.5' Quadrangle (MO) (94) Potosi 7.5' Quadrangle (MO) ST. FRANCOIS COUNTY, MO WASHINGTON COUNTY, MO

Reference Maps

Topographical Map Series (scale 1:250,000). Prepared by the United States Geological Survey.

Dyersburg, Kentucky
Harrison, Arkansas
Rolla, Missouri
Springfield, Missouri

Missouri County Highway Maps. Missouri State Highway Department, Jefferson City, 1992.

Butler	Greene	Texas
Christian	Madison	Washington
Crawford	Ozark	Wayne
Dent	St. Francois	
Douglas	Taney	

Arkansas County Highway Maps. Arkansas State Highway and Transportation Department, Little Rock, 1992.

Baxter	Izard	Randolph
Boone	Lawrence	Sharp
Independence	Marion	Stone

Index

Agriculture: 19, 22–23, 72, 119–20; corn, 23, 54–55, 57, 60, 63, 68, 72–73, 82, 117, 120; cotton, 50, 117, 120; beets, 63; cabbage, 63; onions, 63; turnips, 63; flax, 82, 120; hemp, 82; oats, 83, 117, 126; rye, 83, 117, 120; wheat, 83, 120; tobacco, 117, 120; orchards, 125. *See also* animals, domestic; fences

Animals, domestic: horses, 20, 22, 24–25, 28–29, 38–39, 42–43, 47, 50, 52, 63, 66, 69, 72, 84, 102, 114, packhorse bogged in swamp, 58–59, horses used to find cabin in snow storm, 91–93; dogs, 23, 38, 52, 56, 64, 72, 86, 88, 93; cows, 60, 72, 120; hogs, 60, 72

Animals, wild: elk, 24–25, 40, 48, 82, 84; deer, 25–26, 31, 34, 36, 39, 41–42, 44, 48, 51, 53–54, 56, 62, 64, 74, 76, 79, 82, 84, 86, 96–103; beaver, 26, 51, 67, 89–90; wolves, 26, 72, 79, 42, 84; squirrel, 27, 31, 41–42, 44; buffalo, 30, 48, 50, 53, 56, 66, 73; bears, 31, 38, 40, 42, 44, 48, 54, 55–56, 60, 72, 74, 79, 84, 88; rabbit, 36; panther, 72. *See also* animals, domestic

Arkansas, Territory of: 61, 82, 111, 123

Arkansas Road (Military Road, or Southwest Trail): 27, 112, 159, 161

Artifacts: 100–2

Ashley, Col. William: 28, 31

Ashley's Cave (Saltpeter Cave). *See* caves

Bald-hills. *See* mountains and knobs

Barges: 103

Barrens: 25–26, 145. *See also* prairies

Bellevieu, Mo. *See* cities and towns

Bettis, Dr. (ferry owner on the St. Francis River): 120

Birds: ducks, 26, 31, 41–42, 44, 48, 96; turkeys, 27, 31, 41–42, 44, 48, 56, 58, 62, 73, 79, 82, 84, 96; quail, 36; prairie hen, 42, 81; swan, 42; pigeon, 44; geese, 49, 79,

81, 96; brant, 96; eagle, 96; hawk, 96; heron, 96

Blow-pipe: 75

Boats: keel boats, 47, 60, 83, 103; canoes, 62, 64, 68, 72, 95–96, 99, 117; steamboats, 83, 103

Buffalo Shoals. *See* rapids and shoals

Bull Shoals. *See* rapids and shoals

Bull Shoals Lake: 151, 156

Cabins. *See* dwellings

Calico: 103

Calico Rock (bluff): 109–10

Cane. *See* flora

Canoes. *See* boats

Caves: Ashley's Cave (Saltpeter Cave), 27, 29, 30–31, 51, 119, 146; on Ashley Creek, 28–29; Potato Cave, 44–45, 148; Cathedral Cave, 66, 153; Smallin Cave, 79–81, 154

Christmas, celebration of: 73

Cities and towns: Potosi (Mine à Burton, or Mine à Breton), Mo., 19, 20, 24, 28–29, 32, 53, 93, 98, 112, 125, 143, 164; St. Genevieve, Mo., 19, 120, 124–25; St. Louis, Mo., 19, 25, 61, 98, 111, 116, 120, 124–25; Herculaneum, Mo., 36, 125; St. Charles, Mo., 80; Springfield, Mo. (site of), 82–84, 155; New Orleans, La., 98; Pittsburgh, Penn., 103; Calico Rock, Ark., 109–10, 158; Morrison's Ferry, Ark., 111; Poke Bayou (Batesville), Ark., 111–12, 118; Davidsonville, Ark., 117; Hicks' Ferry (Current View), Mo., 118, 119, 161; Greenville, Mo., 120, 162; Kaskaskia, Ill., 120; Mine La Motte, Mo., 120, 124, 164; St. Michael's (Fredericktown), Mo., 120, 122, 124, 162, 163, 164; Bellevieu, Mo., 122, 124, 126; Cook's Settlement, Mo. (near Farmington), 124; Murphy's Settlement (Farmington), Mo., 124, 164;

Hale's Settlement (Desloge), Mo., 125; Houston, Mo., 146; Raymondville, Mo., 146; Dora, Mo., 148; Tecumseh, Mo., 149; Oldfield, Mo., 154; Norfork, Ark., 157; Calamine, Ark., 159
Clark, William (governor of Missouri Territory): 61
Climate. *See* weather and climate
Clothing: of children, 52–53; leather coats, 53; of women, 54; of foreign manufacture, 60
Commerce: 19–20, 60, 63, 100; potential of the Springfield vicinity, 83; river trader, 98

Dogwood Spring. *See* springs
Dwellings: 22, 52–53, 60, 69. *See also* smoke-house

Earthquakes. *See* New Madrid Earthquake
Edinburgh Reviewer: 38
Education. *See* lifestyles
Elkhorn Spring. *See* springs
Emigrants: 119

Fauna. *See* animals, wild; animals, domestic; birds
Fences: 114
Flora: lichens, 32; moss, 32; black haw, 41, 107; cane, 41–43, 48, 50, 58, 62, 65, 67, 69, 81–82; green briar, 42; shrubs, 42; vines, 42; hackberry, 52, 55; wild hop, 107; wild pea, 107. *See also* trees; prairies
Foods: coffee, 22, 29, 40, 103; venison, 22, 45, 49, 95, 103; honey, 22, 54, 57, 64, 86, 103; bread, 49, 54–55; meat, 49, 53–54, 61–62, 63, 72, 95; pumpkins, 49; acorns, 51, 85; butter, 54; cornbread, 54; preparation of foods, 55–56, 72; bear bacon, 61, 64, 69, 102–3; buffalo beef, 61, 64, 72; potatoes, 63, 83; corn, 69, 72; hominy, 69; tea, 70; bone marrow, 72; beaver tail, 97; flour, 103
Forests. *See* trees
Fossils: 108
Fourche à Courtois (Courtois Creek). *See* rivers and creeks

Geology. *See* rocks and minerals
Glades: 67, 96, 107, 150, 151, 154, 155, 157
Grandosaw River (Osage River). *See* rivers and creeks
Gun powder: 28; manufacture of, 31
Guns. *See* weapons

Hardin's Ferry: 111
Hick's Ferry (Current View), Mo. *See* cities and towns
Hunting and trapping, methods of: 40, 54, 56, 85–86, 88–90
Huzzah Creek (Osage Fork of the Merrimack River). *See* rivers and creeks

Illinois: 19, 76
Indians: 25, 47, 86, 99; hostilities, 23, 60–61; trails (traces), 23, 25, 78; Delaware, 24, 83; Shawnee, 24, 83; Osage, 34, 60–61, 64, 68, 78, 83, 99, 100–1; camps, 47, 49; dwellings, 49, 78; agent, 61; Cherokee, 61, 83; conservation ethic, 78–79; Pawnee, 83, 100; treaty with, 110
Infant death: 74
Iron Mountain. *See* mountains and knobs

Johnson's Bluff: 153
Justice. *See* law and order

Kentucky: 114

Lakes. *See* Prairie of Little Lakes; Norfork Lake; Bull Shoals Lake; Wappapello Lake
Law and order. *See* lifestyles
Lawrence County, Ark.: 54, 112, 117, 119
Lifestyles: of farmers, 23; religion, 32, 42, 73, 110; of hunters, 50, 62–64, 74, 78–79, 88–89, 91–95, 113; law and order, 54, 70–71; of women, 54–55, 62, 74; bargaining, 55; rude pursuits, 55; honesty, 56–57; hospitality, 60; of families, 62–64; schools, 63, 74; of children, 74, 114; marriage, 74; withchcraft and superstition, 74–75, 125; knowledge of the outside world, 98; drinking, 108–9

Madison County, Mo.: 112, 124
Marriage. *See* lifestyles
Medical aid: 39, 74, 114; healing salve, 39; Lee's Pills, 39, 70; for Pettibone, 39; for Schoolcraft, 114–15; muriate of soda, 114
Mine La Motte, Mo. *See* cities and towns
Minerals and rocks: lead (galena), 19–20, 25, 55, 57, 82, 95, 100, 122, 125; limestone, 19–20, 24, 28, 32, 40, 44, 51, 65–66, 71, 76, 80, 82, 101, 105, 108, 110–11, 114, 119–21; pyrite, 20, 33, 51, 122; spars, 20; jasper, 22, 24, 33, 95, 100, 105, 125;

quartz, 22, 24, 32, 33, 51, 95, 101, 105, 108, 121–22, 125; sandstone, 22, 32, 36, 40, 105; carbonate of lime, 24, 95, 104, 108; flint (hornstone), 24, 32–33, 51, 95, 100–2, 105, 125; iron ore, 25, 33, 51, 111, 116, 122; manganese, 25, 33, 117; salt petre, 25, 27–28, 31, 80, 119; calcareous rock, 28, 32, 42, 45, 96, 99, 116, 117, 118, 122, 124–25; clay, 31, 105, 110, 114, 125; nitre, 31; potash, 31; granite, 32, 105, 121–22; slate, 32, 105; silver, 75; rock salt, 100; marble, 101; description of stream pebbles, 104–5; mica, 105, 121; syenite, 105; argillaceous pebbles, 105; gneiss, 105; greenstone, 105, 122; feldspar, 121; blende, 122. See also mining, smelting

Mining: lead, 19–21, 25; on Pearson Creek, 81, 82, 83, 125; tin (reported), 111; iron, 125

Missouri, Territory of: 29, 83, 88, 98, 111, 119, 123

Mitchell, Dr. Samuel L.: 123–24

Mollusks. See fossils

Money: 55, 64, 68, 113; lead as medium of exchange, 19

Mortar and pestle: 55, 69

Mountains and knobs: Sugarloaf Knob, 62, 63; Bald-hill (Helphrey Hill), 76, 91, 153, 155; Pawnee Mountains, 101; Iron Mountain, 122; Round Mountain, 159

Murphy's Settlement (Farmington), Mo. See cities and towns

Narrows of St. Francis. See rapids and shoals, Narrows of the Little St. Francis River

Navigation of rivers: 83, 102–3

New Madrid County, Mo.: 123

New Madrid Earthquake: 122–23

Norfork Lake: 151

North Fork of the White River. See rivers and creeks

Pawnee Mountains. See mountains and knobs

Pettibone, Levi: 20, 29, 57–58, 86; sprained ankle, 39–40; continued toward St. Louis alone, 116, 160

Poke Bayou (Batesville), Ark. See cities and towns

Potosi (Mine à Burton), Mo. See cities and towns

Pottery. See artifacts

Prairies: 35, 47, 77, 80, 85, 145; Prairie of Little Lakes, 25–26; Sugarloaf Prairie, 58, 60–62, 98, 152; Kickapoo Prairie (site of Springfield, Mo.), 82–83. See also flora

Preachers. See lifestyles, religion

Rapids and shoals: Pot Shoals, 98; Bull Shoals 99, 102; Buffalo Shoals, 102; Crooked Creek Shoals, 102; Crooked Rapids, 109; Narrows of St. Francis (Narrows of the Little St. Francis River), 122, 163

Religion. See lifestyles

Rifles. See weapons

Rivers and creeks: Mississippi River, 19–20, 25, 32, 36, 60, 67–68, 73, 82–83, 95, 103–4, 106, 111, 114, 117–18, 120–25; Missouri River, 19, 25, 29, 36, 38, 42, 80, 124; Ohio River, 19, 106; Bates' Creek, 22, 144; Fourche à Courtois (Courtois Creek), 22–24, 31–32, 34, 48, 144; Meramec River, 22, 25, 51, 125; St. Francis River, 22, 25, 120–23, 125; Osage River, 23, 64, 81, 99, 101; White River, 23, 40, 49, 52, 58–61, 65, 74, 76, 79, 81, 83, 88, 90, 92, 93, 96–97, 99, 100, 104–6, 110, 113, 117, 118, 151, 156; Huzzah Creek (Osage Fork of the Merramack River), 24, 144; Current River, 26–27, 29, 51, 117–18, 161; Black River, 27, 29, 47, 117–20, 85, 86, 87, 161; Cave Creek (Ashley Creek), 28–30, 33, 145, 146; Gasconade River, 34, 38, 80; Little Osage River, 38; Muskingum River, 48; Bennett's Bayou, 52, 150; North Fork of the White River, 52, 54–55, 58, 64, 71, 83, 102, 106, 109, 148, 149; Red River, 61; Beaver Creek, 62, 65–66, 96–97, 153, 156; Swan Creek, 78–79, 88, 90; Finley River, 79, 83, 85–86; James River, 80–81, 83–85, 99–100, 106; Bull Creek, 88, 155; Bear Creek, 97; Big Creek, 98; Little North Fork of the White River, 98; Arkansas River, 102, 106, 110; Buffalo River, 102; Crooked Creek, 102; Eleven Point River, 116–18, 167; Spring River, 116–18; Strawberry River, 116–18; Fourche à Thomas (Fourche River), 117–18, 161; Little Black River, 119; Little St. Francis River, 122, 163; Big River, 124; Indian Creek, 147; Panther Creek, 147; West Piney Creek, 147; Cane Creek, 149;

Pearson Creek, 155; Lafferty Creek, 158.
See also navigation of rivers; rapids and
shoals
Rocks. *See* minerals and rocks

Schools. *See* lifestyles
Settlers: Roberts (hunter near Huzzah Creek),
22–24, 25; Well's (on Bennett's Bayou),
52–54, 150; McGary (James McGarrah),
60–61, 65, 97–98, 151, 157; Coker, Lem,
62, 64, 97, 152, 156; Fisher, James, 67–70,
72, 76, 99, 153; Holt, William, 67–69,
71–72, 76, 99, 153; Yochem, Solomon, 97,
102, 156; Friend, Augustine, 100–2; Lee
(Yankee settler below Bull Shoals), 102;
Matney (William), 102, 109, 157; Yochem,
Jacob, 102, 157; Jeffrey (Jehoida), 110;
Lafferty, Widow (widow of John Lafferty),
110, 158; Williams, 110; Bean, Robert,
111; Jones (Stephen Jones), 111, 159;
Wolf, Jacob, 157; Hardin, Joab, 159. *See
also* lifestyles; emigrants
St. Michael's (Fredericktown), Mo. *See* cities
and towns
Shoals. *See* rapids and shoals
Smallin Cave. *See* caves
Smelting: lead, 19–20, 82, 84
Smokehouse: 60–61
Soils: 20, 24, 54, 76, 81–82
South Sea Indian, parable of: 33
Springs: 24; Elkhorn Spring, 41–42; at Potato
Cave, 44; Dogwood Spring, 116, 160;
Kerchner's Spring, 155
Stalactites: 28
Stalagmites: 28
Steamboats. *See* boats
Streams. *See* rivers and creeks
Sugarloaf Prairie. *See* prairies
Superstition. *See* lifestyle
Swamps: 58

Tennessee: 61
Trade. *See* commerce
Trees: Shortleaf Pine *(Pinus echinata),* 22, 26,
28, 43–44, 107, 120; Oak *(Quercus* sp.),
24–26, 28, 36, 38, 41, 47, 51, 76, 80–82,
86, 96; Ash *(Fraxinus americana),* 41, 67,
78, 107; Beech *(Fagus grandifolia),* 41;
Elm *(Ulmus americana),* 41, 78, 81, 89;
Maple *(Acer rubrum),* 41, 67, 78, 81, 89;
Cedar *(Juniperus virginiana),* 67, 96,
107; Mulberry *(Callicarpa americana),*
67, 81, 107; Sassafras *(Laurus sassafras),*
70, 89–90, 107; Hickory *(Carya cordifor-
mus),* 75, 78, 80, 82; *Quercus tinctoria,*
84, 118; Black Walnut *(Juglans nigra),*
107; Buckeye *(Aescuius hippocastanum),*
107; Cottonwood *(Populus angulata),*
107; Crab Apple *(Malus ioensis),* 107;
Dogwood *(cornus floria),* 107, 116;
Pawpaw *(Asinima triloba),* 107;
Persimmon *(Diospyros virginiana),* 107;
Red Elm *(Ulmus fulva),* 107; Red Oak
(Quercus rubra), 107; Sugar Maple *(Acer
saccharum),* 107; Swamp Ash *(Fraxinus
juglandifolia),* 107; White Ash *(Fraxinus
acuminata),* 107; White Elm *(Ulmus
Americana),* 107; White Oak *(Quercus
alba),* 107; White Walnut *(Juglans tomentosa),* 107; Wild Cherry *(Prunus serotina),*
107

Upland flats: 158
Urban growth: 155, 157

Virginia: 114

Wappapello Lake: 162
Washington County, Mo.: 19, 23, 28, 125
Wayne County, Mo.: 112, 119
Weapons: guns, 20, 23, 31, 50, 54, 64; rifles,
23–25, 53, 64, 74, 76, 97
Weather and climate: 27, 51, 58, 65, 81; rain,
25, 31, 51, 58, 71, 73, 90, 120; fog, 50, 51,
71, 88; frost, 66, 69; cold wave, 69; snow,
82, 84, 87–88, 90
Whiskey: 98, 103, 108; distillation of, 12
White River. *See* rivers and creeks